Workplace Writing

PRENTICE HALL
Upper Saddle River, New Jersey
Needham, Massachusetts

ISBN 0-13-435452-4

4 5 6 7 8 9 10   02 01 00 99

PRENTICE HALL

Acknowledgments

Grateful acknowledgment is made to the following for copyrighted material:

Ann Arnott

From "A Woman's Spin: The Main Tenets of Maintenance" by Ann Arnott, featured in *The Detroit Free Press*, 2/1/96. Copyright 1996, Ann Arnott. Reprinted by permission of the author.

Crown Publishers, Inc., a division of Random House

From "Lasting Longer: Cardiorespiratory Fitness" from *The U.S. Army Total Fitness Program* by Dianne Hales and Lt. Col. Robert E. Hales, M.D. Copyright © 1985 by Dianne Hales. Reprinted by permission of Crown Publishers, Inc.

Donadio & Ashworth, Inc.

"Nick Salerno" from *Working* by Studs Terkel. Copyright © 1972, 1974 by Studs Terkel. Reprinted by permission of Donadio & Ashworth, Inc.

The Ebert Co. Ltd.

"Miss Havisham, Minus the Cake" by Roger Ebert, January 30, 1998. Copyright © 1998 The Ebert Co. Ltd. Reprinted by permission of the author.

Gelfand, Rennert & Feldman for Joelsongs

"The Downeaster 'Alexa'" by Billy Joel. Copyright © 1990 Joelsongs. All rights reserved. Used by permission of Gelfand, Rennert & Feldman for Joelsongs.

HarperCollins Publishers Inc.

"Life Stories" by Michael Dorris from *Paper Trail*. Copyright © 1994 by Michael Dorris. All rights reserved. "Teamwork" by Michael Jordan from *I Can't Accept Not Trying: Michael Jordan on the Pursuit of Excellence* by Michael Jordan. Copyright © 1994 by Rare Air, Ltd. Text © 1994 by Michael Jordan. Photographs © 1994 by Sandro Miller. Reprinted by permission of HarperCollins Publishers, Inc.

David Herring

"Photons to Data" (retitled "Measuring Global Climate Changes") by David Herring, EOS-AM Science Outreach Coordinator at NASA Goddard Space Flight Center, Greenbelt, MD. Reprinted by permission of the author.

(Acknowledgments continue on p. 147.)

Contents

Introduction v

Practical and Technical Writing

The Main Tenets of Car Maintenance . . How-to Article 1
   Ann Arnot
Measuring Global Climate Changes . . . Technical Article. 3
   David Herring
Entry-Level Résumés . . . . Résumés 5
Application for Employment . . . . Job Application 7
Driver's License Application . . . . Application. 8
Cardiorespiratory Fitness . . . . Technical Article. 10
   Dianne Hales and Lt. Col. Robert E. Hales, M.D.
Paris: A City Tour by Bus,
   A Gourmet Lunch . . . . Travel Brochure Article 13
      Craig R. Whitney
Municipal Associate Park
   Service Worker . . . . Job Description 15
      Hy Hammer, Ed.
After the Interview . . . . Follow-up Letter 18
   Ronald L. and Caryl Rae Krannich
Title VI of the Clean Air Act . . . . Government Regulations 19
   United States Environmental Protection Agency
Summation for a Jury . . . . Speech. 22
   Cary Bricker

Technology and Communication

Great Expectations . . . . Press Releases 24
   E! Online
Miss Havisham, Minus the Cake . . . . . Movie Review 26
   Roger Ebert
Sister of the Dalai Lama . . . . Radio Interview Transcript . . . 29
   Jetsun Pema with Terry Gross
Finding and Replacing Text . . . . Word Processor User's Guide. . 37
Using the Voice Mail System . . . . Voice Mail User's Guide. 41
Mel Allen: Profile of a Sportscaster . . . . Broadcast Transcript 45
   Scripps Howard News Service

True Stories About First Jobs

The First Appendectomy . . . . Personal Narrative 48
   William A. Nolen
Life Stories . . . . Personal Narrative 54
   Michael Dorris
First Job . . . . Personal Narrative 60
   Maya Angelou

Reflections on a Working Life

Nick Salerno . . . . Reflective Essay 65
   Studs Terkel
Insert Flap "A" and Throw Away . . . . . Humorous Essay 68
   S. J. Perelman

It's Plain Hard Work That Does It . . . . . Biography 72
    Charles Edison
Steelworker . . . . Personal Narrative 78
    Trudy Pax Farr
Teamwork . . . . Reflective Essay 85
    Michael Jordan

Poems, Stories, and Songs About Work

Hephaistos Forges Achilles' Shield . . . . Epic 87
    Homer
Working-Class Hero . . . . Song Lyrics 94
    Alan Jackson and Don Sampson
The Toolmaker Unemployed . . . . Poem 96
    Martin Espada
The Death of the Hired Man . . . . Poem 97
    Robert Frost
The Overcoat . . . . Short Story 102
    Nikolai Gogol
The Downeaster "Alexa" . . . . Song Lyrics 130
    Billy Joel
Growth . . . . Poem 131
    Philip Levine
Assembly Line . . . . Poem 133
    Shu Ting
Those Winter Sundays . . . . Poem 134
    Robert Hayden
The Use of Force . . . . Short Story 135
    William Carlos Williams
The Ballad of John Henry . . . . Song Lyrics 139
    Traditional

Biographical Notes 141

Introduction

The styles and types of workplace writing are as rich and varied as the nature of work itself. Throughout history, people have sung, recited, and written to describe, praise, explain, and facilitate their physical and mental labors. In this collection, you will find a sampling of writing that has been done for and about work.

In the first section, you will read samples of practical and technical writing. When you fill out a form, read a how-to article, or review a job description, you are using practical and technical writing. It is fact-based writing that people use in the workplace or in everyday life. In this section, a how-to article from a newspaper will explain the basic steps needed to keep a car running smoothly. A technical article on measuring global climate changes explains with charts and diagrams how a piece of equipment works. You will learn basic strategies for maintaining a healthy heart in an article from a health handbook, and a travel article outlines the highlights of Paris for a budget-conscious traveler. A job description, an application, and an example of an interview follow-up letter show the kinds of writing you will read and use when you look for a job. Finally, a section of Title VI of the Clean Air Act and a summation for a jury offer examples of specific kinds of writing that people use on the job.

The second section, which deals with technology and communication, contains a variety of selections that show the influence of technology on the way information is conveyed in our society. Press releases are now distributed by electronic mail—like the two press releases about the video versions of *Great Expectations*. Movies are so popular that almost every newspaper in the country carries a movie review feature. Often, they are written by the syndicated movie reviewer Roger Ebert, who wrote the movie review of the 1997 release of *Great Expectations*. Communications for radio and television are recorded in transcripts—word-for-word documentation of what was said on the air. Two transcripts appear in this section: The interview with the Dalai Lama's sister is a radio interview transcript; the profile of Mel Allen is a transcript of a broadcast about the legendary sportscaster.

Real-life work experiences often provide material for entertaining stories or observations about life. The third and fourth sections of this book comprise a number of nonfiction selections that tell true stories about first jobs and offer thoughtful and humorous insights about work. Dr. William A. Nolen takes readers through the trauma of performing a first operation. He describes how his initial confidence deteriorates into incompetence. Michael Dorris and

Maya Angelou share thoughts on the jobs they held as teenagers. In "Nick Salerno," Studs Terkel introduces us to a man who drives a garbage truck; Trudy Pax Farr describes her life as a steel-worker; and Charles Edison describes his father, the man who invented the light bulb. S. J. Perelman's humorous narrative will strike the funny bone of anyone who has ever tried to follow complicated or poorly written directions for items that require some assembly. On a more serious note, Michael Jordan offers words of inspiration that are as relevant to workers in an office building as they are to players on a basketball court.

In the last section, you will read poems, songs, and stories about work. From the classic description of metalwork found in Homer's *Iliad* to Martín Espada's lament for an unemployed toolmaker, the selections in this section offer perspectives on working people and the work they do. In a poem and a short story, Robert Frost and Nikolai Gogol present characters that, although fictional, are representative of working-class people. Alan Jackson and Billy Joel use song lyrics to create personal portraits of an office worker and a fisherman.

Whether you're reading about work or reading text that you might encounter as part of a job, each piece in this collection will increase your understanding of and appreciation for the many activities and skills that are covered under the simple word "work." These selections—like the work that inspires them—will instruct, entertain, challenge, and enrich.

The Main Tenets of Car Maintenance

Ann Arnot

CAR maintenance is getting simpler all the time, thanks to improvements in components, materials and design. But don't become complacent. It's when you let appropriate maintenance slide that things get complicated.

My friend Mike Coley, a mechanic and executive director of technical services for the National Institute for Automotive Service Excellence, tells this story: "I got a call from the owner of a sports car. He had changed the oil at 6,000 miles, but had forgotten about it since then. When I got the call, the car had 16,000 miles on it and the engine had, in essence, frozen. The repair bill was going to be about $1,600."

That's all for want of a $16 oil and filter change. So remember. Though cars are improving both in performance and ease of maintenance, they *do* require upkeep.

Check your owner's manual for your model's specific requirements, and perform these basic checks and changes:

- Tires. At least once a month, check their pressure. Look for signs of uneven wear and cuts and bulges too. Weak spots like those could cause a sudden flat.
- Battery. Inspect for loose connections and corrosion (greenish-white deposits around the terminals) a couple of times a year. If your battery is more than five years old, it's probably running on borrowed time.
- Belts and hoses. These should be checked during oil changes for wear or looseness, and replaced about every four years.
- Exhaust systems. Look for leaks at oil-change time. A leak could allow deadly carbon monoxide to seep into the passenger compartment, causing drowsiness, illness or death.
- Air filter. Get it replaced about every 15,000 miles. A clogged filter could lead to stalling or poor mileage.
- Fuel filter. If your car has fuel injection (most newer models do), have the filter changed about every two years or 30,000 miles.

• Windshield. Periodically make sure your wipers are working and that the windshield-washer fluid reservoir is filled.

• Lights. At least once a year and before every road trip, make sure that all lights, including turn signals and brake lights, are working.

• Oil. This is the lifeblood of your engine. Check it (or have it checked) each time you buy gas. On today's cars, dipsticks are usually clearly marked. Put more in if the mark is below the "add" level.

Change the oil and oil filter every three months or 3,000 miles, whichever comes first. Do this no matter *what* your owner's manual says. Most give two maintenance schedules, for normal and severe driving.

While you may think your driving is normal, this term refers to long, uninterrupted trips at freeway speeds. Most of us drive short distances, with frequent stops and starts.

Following the three-months/3,000-miles rule doesn't cost much and it can go a long way toward preserving your engine.

• Coolant. Check your antifreeze along with the oil. Most cars today have a transparent fluid recovery bottle for easy inspection. If coolant is low, add a 50/50 mixture of antifreeze and water to the recovery tank.

• Transmission fluid. Have it checked at every oil change. Replace it (and the filter) every two years or 24,000 miles.

• Brake fluid. Check whenever the oil is changed, and replace it every two years or 24,000 miles.

• Power-steering fluid. Check at least twice a year and before any long trip.

Measuring Global Climate Changes

David Herring

1.0 Introduction

IN 1998, NASA will begin the primary initiative in its Mission to Planet Earth with the launch of its first Earth Observing System (EOS) satellite. Called EOS AM-1, this satellite will be the first in a series of satellites to fly sensors that will look back at our planet to observe and measure global climate change. The flagship of these sensors will be the Moderate-resolution Imaging Spectroradiometer, or MODIS (see Figure 1). For at least a 15-year period, MODIS instruments will measure visible and infrared light that is either emitted or reflected from every region of the Earth's lands, oceans, and atmosphere.

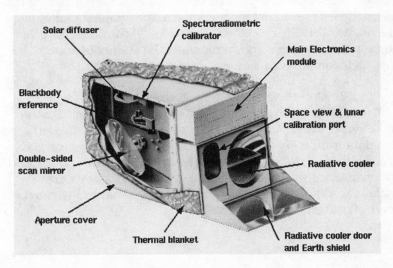

Solar diffuser

Spectroradiometric calibrator

Main Electronics module

Blackbody reference

Space view & lunar calibration port

Double-sided scan mirror

Radiative cooler

Aperture cover

Thermal blanket

Radiative cooler door and Earth shield

2.0 Photons to Data

The flow diagram in Figure 2 illustrates how MODIS converts incoming photons (single units of light) to data. Photons from Earth will pass through MODIS's aperture, a windowlike opening, and hit a constantly spinning, double-sided scan mirror. The scan mirror reflects incoming photons into MODIS's internal telescope, which in turn focuses them onto four different detector assemblies. En route to the detector assemblies, the photons are separated into four broad wavelength ranges: visible light, near infrared, shortwave/midwave infrared, and longwave infrared.

Each time a photon strikes one of the four detectors, an electron is released. Resulting electrons are then converted to digital data. The data are stored aboard MODIS until they can be transmitted to ground receiving stations, where the data will be processed and stored by computers. Using specially developed computer programs, scientists can then translate the data into meaningful images that help them interpret conditions on Earth.

2.1 Onboard Calibrators
In anticipation of the harsh environment of outer space, MODIS instruments will have unprecedented onboard calibration systems, enabling engineers on the ground to monitor the performance throughout their missions. For example, the Spectroradiometric Calibration Assembly (SRCA) is a light source that emits photons at known intensities, which reflect off the scan mirror into the telescope, and proceed through the system. Because the intensities of these photons are known, the scientists know what the readings on the detectors ought to be. If the detectors give incorrect data for these known photons, the scientists know to adjust their computer processes to correct their data.

3.0 Conclusion
The MODIS instruments will be the best calibrated Earth remote sensors ever launched. They will provide much-needed spectral data from every region on Earth for at least 15 years. Ultimately, these data will help scientists better understand the Earth as a whole, integrated system so that they may assist policymakers worldwide to manage and protect our natural resources more effectively and more efficiently.

Entry-Level Résumé

Regina A. Washington

LOCAL ADDRESS
40 Cortney Street, Apt. D-2
East Lansing, MI 23958
(615) 342-9837

PERMANENT ADDRESS
12 Plumtree Circle
Media, PA 19485
(610) 366-9382

EDUCATION

Michigan State University, Master of Science in Management with a concentration in Human Resource Management Candidate, May 1998.

Bucknell University, Bachelor of Science, Major: Psychology, May 1995.

Bucknell University Studies Abroad Program, Cortona, Italy. Marble sculpting and drawing, June–August 1994.

EXPERIENCE

Graduate Assistant, Department of Management, Michigan State University (September 1996–present)—assist two professors, including the Department Head of Management, in research.

Intern, The Hay Group, Philadelphia, PA, HR management consulting firm (Spring 1995–Summer 1995)—organization of job satisfaction surveys and result, compiling self-help packets for feedback, marketing research (Christmas 1996)—co-wrote report on HR strategies for Workforce 2000.

Assistant in Operations, GraphTech, Inc., Malvern, PA (Spring 1994, Fall 1994)—graphic design, training documentation development, software testing, electronic forms design (Christmas 1992, Fall 1993)—receptionist.

Tutor, Bucknell University (Fall 1992, Spring 1993)—tutored students in software use, computer hardware installation, troubleshooting.

HONORS AND ACTIVITIES

Graduate Women's Business Network, Treasurer
MBA/MS Association Member
Dean's Honor List, Honor List
Allison Meyers Scholarship, 4 years
USSR Friendship Force Exchange
Catalyst Committee Chair
Intramural Assoication, board member
Artwork selected for 25th Annual Mostra, Cortona, Italy

COMPUTER SKILLS

PC DOS: Lotus 123, dBase, WordPerfect, MSWord, Wordstar
MACINTOSH: PageMaker, Microsoft Word, MacWrite, MacDraw

GRADUATION May 1998

Entry-Level Résumé

Laura A. Kelleter

LOCAL ADDRESS
P.O. Box 14
East Lansing, MI 13948
(415) 437-9473

PERMANENT ADDRESS
18 Tyler Lane
Green Bay, WI 13958
(615) 433-9374

EDUCATION

Michigan State University, Master of Science in Human Resource Management expected May 1998; current GPA 3.75

Penn State University, Bachelor of Arts in English and Spanish, May 1996; Graduated with Honors—completed 36 hours of Honors Courses; GPA 3.4

EXPERIENCE

Summer Intern, Human Resources, Johnson & Johnson, New Brunswick, NJ—Worked on Equal Employment Opportunity and Team Effectiveness projects (Summer 1997)

Graduate Assistant, Department of Management, Michigan State University—Compiled a mailing list of Human Resource Executives to be used in a department research project; reviewed textbook galleys; assisted in grading tests (September 1996–present)

Summer Intern, Human Resources, Dow Chemical Company, Midland, MI—Developed and moderated a New Employee Orientation Program; identified issues and impacts of the current disability reporting process and made recommendations to improve the process; coordinated tours, activities, and weekly lunch speakers for summer interns (May 1996–August 1996)

Tour Guide and Desk Worker, Visitor Center, Michigan State University—Scheduled visitor appointments; showed prospective students around campus (September 1994–May 1996)

Summer Intern, Human Resources, Scott Paper Company, Philadelphia, PA—Coordinated the summer intern program, including tours and activities, and compiled a manual for the coordination of this program; developed supervisor guidelines outlining pre-arrival steps and a summer timetable for supervisors of summer interns; interpreted data from recruiting surveys (May 1995–August 1995)

HONORS AND ACTIVITIES

* Honors Graduate, Penn State University, 1996
* Who's Who Among Students in American Universities and Colleges
* Student Government: Freshman Programs (Outstanding Freshman Aide)
* Parents' Weekend Committee Programming Sub-Chairman for 2 years
* Mortar Board, Inc./Cap & Gown (Publicity Chairman)—National Senior Honor Society
* Cardinal Key/Tau Kappa Chapter—National Junior Honor Society
* Freshman Program—planned activities to assist incoming freshmen with their transition from high school to college

GRADUATION   May 1998

Application for Employment

Name (Last, First, Middle)

Address (Street and Number, City, State, Zip)

Home Phone   School or Business Phone   Social Security Number

Please describe the position you are seeking.

Education

Schools Attended _____

Current Level of Education _____

Scholastic Honors and Awards _____

_____

Interests and Activities _____

_____

Employment Experience List all employment in the past three years, beginning with your most recent position. _____

_____

_____

Office Skills

Word Processing: ☐ Yes ☐ No Typing: ☐ Yes ☐ No (w.p.m.) ____

List all computer programs you can use. _____

_____

References Please give the names, addresses, and telephone numbers of two references (note: references cannot be relatives).

_____

_____

_____

Driver's License Application

Application for:
_____Driver's License
_____Instruction Permit
_____Commercial Driver's License
_____Commercial Driver's License Instruction Permit
_____Personal ID Card

_____Check here if you want to be an organ donor.

If you have a driver's license from another state, enter the
license number and state here:_____

Social Security Number_____ Sex ____ Date of Birth ____

Full Legal Name
Last Name   First Name   Middle or Maiden Name
_____

Any Prior Legal Name _____

Residence Address _____

City or County of Residence _____

City_____ State _____ Zip Code _____

Mailing Address (If different from above)
Street _____ City _____

State _____ Zip Code _____

Weight _____ Height _____ Eye Color _____ Hair Color _____

Do you wear glasses or contact lenses?   Y   N

Do you have a physical or mental condition
that requires that you take medication?   Y   N

Have you ever had a seizure, blackout,
or loss of consciousness?   Y   N

Do you have a physical condition that requires
you to use special equipment in order to drive?   Y   N

Have you been convicted within the past
10 years in this state or elsewhere or any offense
resulting from your operation of, or involving,
a motor vehicle? (Do not include parking tickets.)   Y   N

Is or has your license or privilege to drive ever been
suspended, revoked, or disqualified in this state
or elsewhere?   Y   N

If you answered YES to any of the above questions, please explain.

_____

_____

I certify that all information given in this application is true and
correct to the best of my knowledge. I understand that it is unlawful for any applicant to knowingly make a false statement on
an application.

Applicant's Signature _____

Cardiorespiratory Fitness

Dianne Hales and Lt. Col. Robert E. Hales, M.D.

Conditioning Your Heart and Lungs: How Much Is Enough?

YOUR heart and lungs need regular work in order to reach peak efficiency. Most activities that involve the major muscles of the body can condition them, but in order to get the full benefits from your efforts, you have to exercise often, hard, and long enough.

How hard do you have to work? That depends on the shape you're in. If you haven't been exercising regularly, even mild forms of exertion, such as a brisk walk, can seem rigorous. As you get in shape, your body will be able to handle much greater challenges.

Your heart rate is the best monitor of how hard you're working. You don't need to go to your absolute limit, but you should raise your heart rate to 60 to 75 percent of your maximum; this is your target heart rate. To find your target rate in the following table, look for the age category closest to your age and read the lines across. For example, if you

TARGET HEART RATE Beats per minute		
Age	Average Maximum Rate (100%)	Target Rate (60–75%)
20	200	120 – 150
25	195	117 – 146
30	190	114 – 142
35	185	111 – 138
40	180	108 – 135
45	175	105 – 131
50	170	102 – 127
55	165	99 – 123
60	160	96 – 120
65	155	93 – 116
70	150	90 – 113

Source: *Family Fitness Handbook*, Soldier Physical Fitness Center, Fort Benjamin Harrison, Indianapolis

are 30, your target rate is 114 to 142 beats per minute. If you are 43, the closest age on the chart is 45; the target rate is 105 to 131 beats per minute.

If you don't push to at least 60 percent, you're not really helping yourself. If you push beyond 90 percent, you could be hurting yourself. In the initial stages of training, aim for the lower part of your target zone, gradually building up from 60 to 75 percent of your maximum heart rate. After six months or more of regular exercise, you can push harder if you wish—although you don't have to just to stay in condition. As long as your target heart rate is your guide, your exercise intensity should be

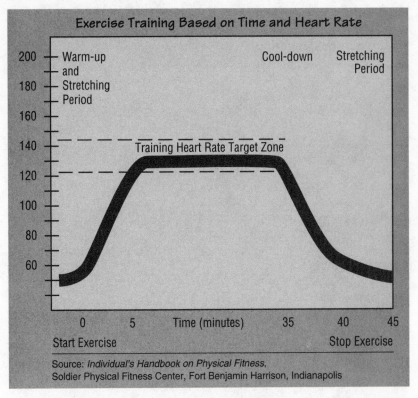

Source: *Individual's Handbook on Physical Fitness*,
Soldier Physical Fitness Center, Fort Benjamin Harrison, Indianapolis

neither too low nor too high, but just right.

How long should you exercise? A stroll around the block may lift your spirits; a sprint over the same distance makes your heart beat faster. But neither produces lasting results. You need to work out for at least 20 minutes—and the Army's found that 30 minutes of aerobic exercise provides the maximum benefits.

How often should you exercise? If you exercise only once or twice a week, you can increase your aerobic capacity (your body's ability to use oxygen) by about 8 percent. If you work out three times a week—the minimum recommended—your aerobic capacity should improve by 15 percent. Four weekly workouts should produce a 25 percent improvement: After that, improvements level off. For optimal benefits, the Army encourages its soldiers to do aerobic exercises four days a week.

How much is too much? In the 1960s, when Dr. Cooper, then an Air Force physician, was developing the concept of aerobics, he believed that since some exercise was very good, more had to be better. That's not necessarily so. Beyond a certain point, risks outdistance benefits. "Running more than 15 to 20 miles a week doesn't make you any more fit," Cooper now comments, "and it can be dangerous."

Paris: A City Tour by Bus, A Gourmet Lunch

Craig R. Whitney

ONE of the few things in Paris that has become less expensive, even before the dollar began surging toward 6 francs, is a bus ride. Long routes that used to require two tickets now cost just 8 francs (about $1.40, based on 5.74 francs to the dollar) if a single ticket is bought on the bus or 4.80 francs (about 85 cents) if a carnet of 10 is bought at a Metro station. This makes a ride on the scenic No. 63, from the Gare de Lyon in the east of the city to the Porte de la Muette on its western edge, the biggest bargain in town.

After you punch your ticket in the validating machine inside the bus, the journey begins as you leave the Gare de Lyon and cross the Seine on the Pont d'Austerlitz to the Left Bank, providing a fine view of the apse of Notre-Dame. It continues west to the eastern end of the Boulevard St.-Germain, doglegging into the Latin Quarter toward the College de France, the Sorbonne and the Cluny Museum.

The route then crosses the Boulevard St.-Michel, past the Odeon Theater, to the Rue St.-Sulpice, past the 17th-Century church of the same name, to the Boulevard Raspail.

There it rejoins the Boulevard St.-Michel and then the Seine, following the river westward past the National Assembly and the Quai d'Orsay, with fine views of the Invalides and the Eiffel Tower before crossing to the Right Bank at the Place de l'Alma. It climbs to the Place du Trocadero with another splendid view, and then peters out along the Avenue Henri Martin to the western terminus.

Going the other way, the route continues straight along the Boulevard St.-Michel for its length. Buses become few and far between after the evening rush hour and stop altogether about 10 p.m. Intermediate stations along the route, like either terminus, are marked with little "63" signs and provide timetables. If you start at a terminus you're guaranteed a window seat.

One of these stops—the Place du Trocadero—is within walking distance of Alain Ducasse's celebrated and expensive restaurant on the Avenue Raymond Poincare in the 16th Arrondissement. Though the rallying dollar has made Paris merely expensive, instead of ridiculously expensive, Ducasse remains quite a splurge.

But the lunch menu holds some relative bargains, such as the four-course prix fixe lunch, which varies with the seasons, at 480 francs (about $84), or only 100 bus rides. A sample menu: a delicious salad of fresh cold asparagus, turnips, carrots, mushrooms and greens in olive oil, continuing through Volaille de Bresse (poultry from Bresse) with long, hollow pasta accompanied by white truffles, cheese and dessert.

Restaurant Alain Ducasse is at 59 Avenue Raymond Poincare, 75116 Paris. It's closed Saturdays, Sundays, Dec. 24 to Jan. 4, and July 15 to Aug. 15.

Municipal Associate Park Service Worker

Hy Hammer, Editor

Job Description

UNDER supervision, operates and maintains various types of motorized equipment; performs groundskeeping or gardening work in any park area required including all work in connection with the planting, maintenance, and removal of trees and large shrubs; inspects and performs general maintenance and repair work to buildings, monuments, and similar works of art, equipment, and facilities; and/or serves as an operator in a chlorination, coagulation, and/or filtration plant; performs related work.

Examples of Typical Tasks. Performs all aspects of gardening work including grading, cultivating, fertilizing, seeding, laying sod, mowing, and trimming hedges; sweeping and raking litter and emptying receptacles; planting, cultivating, and caring for trees, flowers, plants, shrubs, and other flora; and operates and cares for hand and power gardening tools and equipment. Operates cars, trucks, and other motorized equipment incidental to the performance of duties and/or operates heavy-duty motorized equipment on a full-time basis; checks vehicles to ensure they are in proper operating condition; changes tires and performs routine servicing. Cleans dirt accumulation and debris from monuments. Assists in or performs general repair work. Assists in climbing and pruning work; and may operate manual power driven equipment in the performance of these duties. Operates and maintains a chlorination, coagulation, and/or filtration plant consisting of chlorine and/or coagulation machine and auxiliary equipment used in purification and chemical treatment of water. Operates a low-pressure heating system; cleans and lubricates the boiler parts. Performs any necessary record-keeping and report writing activities related to the above functions of the Department of Parks and Recreation.

Requirements

1. High school graduation or evidence of having passed an examination for a high school equivalency diploma and six months of full-time paid experience in gardening, grounds maintenance, or in the building construction or maintenance trades; or

2. Two years of full-time paid experience in gardening, grounds maintenance, or in the building construction or maintenance trades; or

3. One year of full-time paid experience as a climber or pruner or tree worker performing climber and tree pruning duties; or

4. A satisfactory equivalent combination of (1) and/or (2) and/or (3) above.

License. At the time of appointment, eligibles must possess a valid commercial driver's license for the operation of trucks and tractors in excess of 18,000 pounds, maximum gross weight (MGW). If the license was issued in a state which did not require a road test with a vehicle in excess of 18,000 pounds MGW, the eligible will be required to demonstrate ability to operate such vehicles to the satisfaction of the appointing officer.

Test Information

Written, weight 100, 70% required. The written test will be of the multiple-choice type and may include questions in the following areas: rudimentary gardening techniques; park area and park building maintenance; cleaning of park, playground, and comfort stations; maintenance of tennis courts, beaches, ball fields, golf courses, and other recreation areas; defensive driving and minor automotive servicing techniques; rudimentary painting and repair techniques including the maintenance of tools; reading and understanding simple instructional materials; the writing of short, simple reports of accidents; arithmetic (addition and subtraction); basic first aid techniques; chlorination and filtration plant operation and low-pressure heating plant operation; and supervision of employees.

Qualifying Physical Tests. Medical evidence to allow participation in the physical test may be required, and the Department of Personnel reserves the right to exclude from the physical test eligibles who, upon examination of such evidence, are apparently medically unfit. Eligibles will take the physical test at their own risk of injury, although every effort will be made to safeguard them. Eligibles will be required to satisfactorily complete the following physical test consisting of two subtests:

1. *Strength subtest.* Eligibles must lift a bag weighing approximately 50 pounds from the floor, place it on a table approximately four feet in height, and then return the bag to the floor under control. The eligible will be required to perform this operation for a total of eight times within three minutes.
2. *Agility subtest.* Eligibles must first climb three steps to a foothold 44 inches high, then step or climb over a 26 inch wall to a platform. The eligible must then descend to the ground by stepping or climbing back over the wall and climbing down to the ground. Eligibles will be required to complete this subtest within three minutes. Eligibles will be given two attempts to complete each subtest.

Qualifying Medical. An eligible will be rejected for any medical condition which impairs his or her ability to perform the duties of Associate Park Service Worker. Periodic reexamination will be required.

Advancement
Associate Park Service Workers are afforded the promotion opportunity, when eligible, to the title of Park Supervisor.

After the Interview

Ronald L. and Caryl Rae Krannich

9910 Thompson Drive
Cleveland, OH 43382

June 21, 19__

Jane Evans, Director
EVANS FINANCE CORPORATION
2122 Forman Street
Cleveland, OH 43380

Dear Ms. Evans:

Your advice was most helpful in clarifying my questions on careers in finance. I am now reworking my résumé and have included many of your thoughtful suggestions. I will send you a copy next week.

Thanks so much for taking time from your busy schedule to see me. I will keep in contact and follow through on your suggestion to see Sarah Cook about opportunities with the Cleveland-Akron Finance Company.

Sincerely,

Daryl Haines

Daryl Haines

Title VI of the Clean Air Act

United States Environmental Protection Agency

SEC. 609. SERVICING OF MOTOR VEHICLE AIR CONDITIONERS.

(a) REGULATIONS. Within one year after the enactment of the Clean Air Act Amendments of 1990, the Administrator shall promulgate regulations in accordance with this section establishing standards and requirements regarding the servicing of motor vehicle air conditioners.

(b) DEFINITIONS. As used in this section

(1) The term 'refrigerant' means any class I or class II substance used in a motor vehicle air conditioner. Effective five years after the enactment of the Clean Air Act Amendments of 1990, the term 'refrigerant' shall also include any substitute substance.

(2) (A) The term 'approved refrigerant recycling equipment' means equipment certified by the Administrator (or an independent standards testing organization approved by the Administrator) to meet the standards established by the Administrator and applicable to equipment for the extraction and reclamation of refrigerant from motor vehicle air conditioners. Such standards shall, at a minimum, be at least as stringent as the standards of the Society of Automotive Engineers in effect as of the date of the enactment of the Clean Air Act Amendments of 1990 and applicable to such equipment (SAE standard J-1990).

(B) Equipment purchased before the proposal of regulations under this section shall be considered certified if it is substantially identical to equipment certified as provided in subparagraph (A).

(3) The term 'properly using' means, with respect to approved refrigerant recycling equipment, using such equipment in conformity with standards established by the Administrator and applicable to the use of such equipment. Such standards shall, at a minimum, be at least as stringent as the standards of the Society of Automotive Engineers in effect as of the date of the enactment of the Clean Air Act Amendments of 1990 and applicable to the use of such equipment (SAE standard J-1989).

19

(4) The term 'properly trained and certified' means training and certification in the proper use of approved refrigerant recycling equipment for motor vehicle air conditioners in conformity with standards established by the Administrator and applicable to the performance of service on motor vehicle air conditioners. Such standards shall, at a minimum, be at least as stringent as specified, as of the date of the enactment of the Clean Air Act Amendments of 1990, in SAE standard J-1989 under the certification program of the National Institute for Automotive Service Excellence (ASE) or under a similar program such as the training and certification program of the Mobile Air Conditioning Society (MACS).

(c) SERVICING MOTOR VEHICLE AIR CONDITIONERS. Effective January 1, 1992, no person repairing or servicing motor vehicles for consideration may perform any service on a motor vehicle air conditioner involving the refrigerant for such air conditioner without properly using approved refrigerant recycling equipment and no such person may perform such service unless such person has been properly trained and certified. The requirements of the previous sentence shall not apply until January 1, 1993, in the case of a person repairing or servicing motor vehicles for consideration at an entity which performed service on fewer than 100 motor vehicle air conditioners during calendar year 1990 and if such person so certifies, pursuant to subsection (d) (2), to the Administrator by January 1, 1992.

(d) CERTIFICATION. (1) Effective two years after the enactment of the Clean Air Amendments of 1990, each person performing service on motor vehicle air conditioners for consideration shall certify to the Administrator either

(A) that such person has acquired, and is properly using, approved refrigerant recycling equipment in service on motor vehicle air conditioners involving refrigerant and that each individual authorized by such person to perform such service is properly trained and certified; or

(B) that such person is performing such service at an entity which serviced fewer than 100 motor vehicle air conditioners in 1991.

(2) Effective January 1, 1993, each person who certified under paragraph (1) (B) shall submit a certification under paragraph (1) (A).

(3) Each certification under this subsection shall contain the name and address of the person certifying under this subsection

and the serial number of each unit of approved recycling equipment acquired by such person and shall be signed and attested by the owner or another responsible officer. Certifications under paragraph (1) (A) may be made by submitting the required information to the Administrator on a standard form provided by the manufacturer of certified refrigerant recycling equipment.

(e) SMALL CONTAINERS OF CLASS I OR CLASS II SUBSTANCES. Effective two years after the date of the enactment of the Clean Air Act Amendments of 1990, it shall be unlawful for any person to sell or distribute, or offer for sale or distribution, in interstate commerce to any person (other than a person performing service for consideration on motor vehicle air-conditioning systems in compliance with this section) any class I or class II substance that is suitable for use as a refrigerant in a motor vehicle air-conditioning system and that is in a container which contains less than 20 pounds of such refrigerant.

Summation for a Jury

Cary Bricker

LADIES and Gentlemen of the jury:

This is a case about a young woman, Anna Shepard, accused of a bank robbery she did not commit. This is a case about mistaken identity. This is a case about an innocent person, falsely accused.

As we turn to the prosecution's case, ask yourselves whether the testimony of its two witnesses raised many more questions than it provided answers. Did their testimony leave you wondering who the real perpetrator might be? Did it make you wish the police had been more diligent in their investigation of this case? If so, then you have clear, reasonable doubts—reasons you must acquit.

Recall first the testimony of Allen Parker, the bank teller at First Federal Savings on the morning of the robbery. He provided you with a description of the real perpetrator, the woman who came to his counter, displayed what was later identified as a toy gun, and demanded $500 in small bills. He described a dark-haired woman of five feet seven and approximately one hundred seventy pounds. He explained that she was wearing a red bandanna, which covered three quarters of her face.

Contrast that description with arresting officer John Hendricks's description of Anna Shepard. Her hair, he said, was dirty blond, and she carried one hundred thirty-five pounds on her five-feet-four-inch frame. Where the chief eye witness's description of the person who robbed him is significantly different from that of the accused, that is the very definition of reasonable doubt—reason you must acquit.

Officer Hendricks also testified that the reason he arrested Anna was because she was running away from the front door of First Federal Savings moments after the bank's alarm sounded. But recall during my cross-examination how he admitted that he was only around the corner when he first heard the alarm. Remember that Anna had neither paper money nor a bandanna on her when he searched her seconds later. There is simply no way that Ms. Shepard could have hidden away $500 and a red bandanna between the time of the robbery and the time of her arrest. Why, at the moment of her arrest, did she possess only a small purse containing change, a bank card, and keys? Because she is an innocent woman, falsely accused.

Officer Hendricks explained that the bank has a back door, through which the true robber could have escaped without being noticed during the commotion up front. He admitted that no one, official or otherwise, was stationed at the back door to stop someone fleeing the scene. Remember, too, that he recovered the very toy gun that Allen Parker had identified as the robber's from the floor near that back door. More reasonable doubt—reason you must acquit this innocent woman.

Lastly, recall the testimony of Anna Shepard herself. Because the prosecutors have the only burden of proof in this criminal trial, Anna could have stayed in her seat and relied on the weakness of their case to establish her innocence. But she wanted to talk to you, to describe the horror of being accused of a crime she did not commit. Anna described how she headed for the market, stopping first at First Federal's ATM to get shopping money. As she approached the machine, she heard screaming from inside the bank, followed by the alarm. She reacted as anyone else would have under the circumstances: Fearing that a robbery was occurring, and concerned that the robber might have a gun, she ran at top speed away from the bank. Someone yelled out, "Stop her!" just as Officer Hendricks rounded the corner. Anna explained to you how the officer grabbed her right on the spot, but did not talk to potential witnesses to ensure he was arresting the robber and not a young woman who happened to be at the wrong place at the wrong time.

Ms. Shepard told you of what followed—her arrest, the nightmare of being taken to the police station in handcuffs, of being treated like a criminal and robbed of her dignity.

Members of the jury, as you retire to deliberate, please take this case as seriously as you would if a loved one sat where Anna Shepard now sits. If you use your common sense when reviewing the evidence and hold the prosecutor to his burden of proof beyond a reasonable doubt, we have no question that you will end Anna Shepard's nightmare by finding her not guilty.

Thank you.

Great Expectations (1946)

E! Online

Category:	Drama
Director:	*David Lean*
Cast:	*John Mills*
	Alec Guinness
	Valerie Hobson
	Jean Simmons
	Martita Hunt
Run Time:	118 (mins)
Rating:	NR
Distributor Name:	Malofilm Group
Country:	United Kingdom
Summary:	In the gloom of a country graveyard, a young boy encounters an escaped convict, a chance meeting that years later leads the boy to mystery, wealth and joy in this Charles Dickens classic. Academy Award Nominations: 5, including Best Picture, Best Director, Best Screenplay.

Great Expectations (1978)

E! Online

Category:	Drama
Director:	*Julian Amyes*
Cast:	*Gerry Sundquist* *Stratford Johns*
Run Time:	72 (mins)
Rating:	NR
Distributor Name:	20th Century Fox Home Entertainment
Summary:	Charles Dickens's story of humble village boy who is orphaned at an early age. He is brought up by his domineering sister and her blacksmith husband. The story follows his journey through boyhood and into the fine life he has made for himself in London. His callous behavior catches up to him as he is faced with the discovery of his true self. A BBC production.

Miss Havisham, Minus the Cake

Roger Ebert

THIS is not, says Finn, the way the story really happened, but the way he remembers it. That is how everyone tells the stories that matter to them: Through their own eyes, rewritten by their own memories, with bold underscores for the parts that hurt. Finn's story is the life of a poor boy who falls in love with a rich girl who has been trained since childhood to break the hearts of men.

This tale has been borrowed from Charles Dickens' "Great Expectations," where it is told in less lurid images and language, to be sure, but with the same sense of an innocent boy being lured into the lair of two dangerous women. That the women are lonely, sad, and good at heart makes it bittersweet.

"What is it like not to feel anything?" Finn shouts at Estella after she has abandoned him.

Of course, if you cannot feel anything, that is exactly the question you cannot answer.

The story has been updated by director Alfonso Cuaron, who moves it from Victorian England to a crumbling neo-Gothic mansion in Florida. It stars Ethan Hawke as Finn (Pip in the book), and Gwyneth Paltrow as Estella, the beautiful niece of the eccentric millionairess Ms. Dinsmoor (Anne Bancroft).

Their paths cross in one of those backwaters of Florida that have been immortalized by writers like Elmore Leonard and John D. MacDonald, where creeping condos from the north have not yet dislodged small fishing shacks and the huge masonry pile of Paradiso Perduto, which once was a glittering showplace but is now engulfed in trees and creepers, and falling into decay.

Finn lives with his sister Maggie and "her man," Joe (Chris Cooper), who raises him after Maggie disappears. One day he is seen by Ms. Dinsmoor, who invites him to Paradiso Perduto to play with her niece. The two children are about 10. Finn is a gifted artist, and as he sketches the young girl, the old crone perceives that he will eventually fall in love with the girl, and sees her chance for revenge against men.

The original Ms. Dinsmoor is, of course, Miss Havisham, one of the most colorful and pathetic characters in Dickens, who was left stranded on her wedding day by a faithless lover. This version of "Great Expectations" spares us the sight of her wedding cake, covered in cobwebs after the decades (in Florida, tiny visitors would make short work of that feast). But it succeeds in making Ms. Dinsmoor equally sad and venomous, and Anne Bancroft's performance is interesting: Despite the weird eye makeup and the cigarettes, despite the flamboyant clothing, she is human, and not without humor.

"That's the biggest cat I've ever seen," Finn says on his first visit. "What do you feed it?" She waits for a beat. "Other cats," she says.

Paradiso Perduto and its inhabitants reminded me of "Grey Gardens," the 1976 documentary about two relatives of Jackie Onassis, who lived in a decaying mansion in East Hampton with countless cats. There is the same sense of defiance: If I was once young, rich, and beautiful, these women say to the world, see what you have made of me!

Cuaron, whose previous film was "The Little Princess," brings a touch of magic realism to the setting, with weeping willows, skies filled with sea birds, and a scene where Finn and Estella dance to "Besame Mucho" while Ms. Dinsmoor looks on, cold-eyed.

Time passes. The young actors who played Finn and Estella are replaced by Hawke and Paltrow, who meet again at the mansion after several years, and share a sudden kiss at a water fountain, which is cut between backlit shots from moving cameras so that it seems more orgiastic than most sex scenes.

After this romantic spark Estella again dances away, and the story continues some years later in New York, where a mysterious benefactor offers to bankroll Finn's show at an important gallery, and Estella again appears on the scene, this time with a hapless fiance-victim named Walter in tow.

"Great Expectations" begins as a great movie (I was spellbound by the first 30 minutes), but ends as only a good one, and I think that's because the screenplay, by Mitch Glazer, too closely follows the romantic line. Dickens, who of course had more time and space to move around in, made it the story of a young man's coming of age, and the colorful characters he encountered—from the escaped prisoner of the opening scenes (played here by Robert De Niro) to good old, proud old Joe. The moment this movie declares itself as being mostly about affairs of the heart, it limits its potential.

And yet the film is a successful translation of the basic material from one period and approach to another. Especially in the early

Florida scenes, it seems timeless. Hawke and Paltrow project that uneasy alertness of two people who know they like one another and suspect they'll regret it.

But the subplot involving the escaped prisoner doesn't really pay off (it feels more like a bone thrown to Dickens than a necessity of the plot). And I am not quite sure that any good artist can create only when he's in sync with the girl of his dreams: Some artists paint best when their hearts are broken, and most artists paint no matter what, because they have to.

"Great Expectations" doesn't finish at the same high level that it begins (if it did, it would be one of the year's best films), but it's visually enchanted; the cinematographer, Emmanuel Lubezki, uses lighting and backlighting like a painter. And the characters have more depth and feeling than we might expect in what is, underneath everything, a fantasy. There's great joy in a scene where Finn sweeps Estella out of a restaurant and asks her to dance. And sadness later as she observes that Ms. Dinsmoor's obsessions have become her own.

Sister of the Dalai Lama

Jetsun Pema with Terry Gross

TERRY GROSS, HOST. This is FRESH AIR. I'm Terry Gross.

My guest Jetsun Pema is the younger sister of the Dalai Lama. They're both dedicated to keeping alive Tibetan culture and religion, despite the Chinese occupation in which over 100,000 Tibetan monks and nuns have been killed or tortured.

Jetsun Pema grew up in Tibet and now lives in exile in Dharamsala, India, which is the seat of the Tibetan government in exile. She heads the Tibetan Children's Village, which educates exiled Tibetan children about their culture and religion. She was the first woman minister of the Tibetan government in exile, and was awarded the title "Mother of Tibet" by its national assembly.

Some of her family's story is told in the film *Seven Years in Tibet* and *Kundun*, Martin Scorcese's new movie which opens Christmas Day. Pema tells her own story in her new autobiography.

When she was born in 1940, her brother was already recognized as the Dalai Lama. I asked if, as a child, she was expected to behave a certain way in his presence.

JETSUN PEMA, "MOTHER OF TIBET," AUTHOR, *TIBET: MY STORY,* HEAD, TIBETAN CHILDREN'S VILLAGE. You know, His Holiness was already recognized and he was installed in the Potala. And so as a child, I always knew that I had a brother who was living up in the Potala.

GROSS. That's the palace?

PEMA. Yes, that's the palace. It's a —you know, it's up on a hill and it's very impressive. There's over thousands of—a thousand rooms. And it overlooks the little town of Lhasa. And when you heard your mother saying, you know, "His Holiness is living up there," I think it gave you the impression that he was very special.

And so whenever we went up those flights of stairs to go and see him, and he had all the—you know, his monk attendants around him. And my mother and father would prostrate in front of him. And so, we also had to do that.

And with all that kind of, sort of, you know ceremony just to go and see him, I think it put a message in my head that he was somebody special, and somebody who had to be treated with great respect.

GROSS. Do you ever think what it was like for your parents to have their baby boy be "His Holiness" and to have to bow when they saw him?

PEMA. Well, for any Tibetan family, you know, for a Tibetan, parents to have their son recognized as a reincarnate lama—it's a great privilege and an honor, because Tibetans by nature are very religious, and our religion is very important in our lives. It's not just religion as such, but it's become a way of life for the Tibetans.

So when you have a reincarnate lama as your son, I think parents are really awed by that, and they are—they feel that it's an honor and they pay great respect to their incarnate, you know, reincarnate lama son.

GROSS. You were born about nine years before China invaded Tibet, and the way of life in Tibet was changed. Would you share with us some of your memories of life in Tibet before the Chinese invasion? Just about what day to day life was like for you?

PEMA. Well, for me, being born after His Holiness was recognized, you know, we had all the special privileges. My parents came from a little village in eastern Tibet. They were, you know, just farmers. And they—all of a sudden, the Dalai Lama is discovered in their family, and then they were brought to Lhasa, to the capital of Tibet. And there they were given whatever they needed and they were, you know, a new—big new house was built for them.

And I grew up in this. You know, I was born after His—one year later. And I grew up with my young—with my sister's children, a boy and a girl. And then many of our servants, they had their children and we had a wonderful time.

So my memories of Tibet was always always very happy memories, where we had just wonderful times and, you know, playing with our—with my nephew and niece and the children of the servants. Then going to school to learn to read and write Tibetan. And also, you know, visiting the various monasteries and enjoying the various festivals that were celebrated in the city of Lhasa.

So, I think I just have just wonderful memories of Tibet.

GROSS. What do you think your parents expected that your life would be like when you grew up? Before the invasion?

PEMA. Oh, well, if—if the Chinese didn't come to Tibet and, you know, then I think I might have stayed on in Lhasa and just got a Tibetan education and stayed on. But then because the Chinese entered Tibet at the end of 1949, then my sister—my older sister—she was also not feeling well, and my mother decided that we should accompany her to India and to remain in India to get an education.

And along with me, my sister's two children, they also came. And so the three of us, we were sent with my sister to India to study.

GROSS. So you were sent to India for your education, as a girl, and I believe you were educated in a Catholic convent. What was it like for you, as a Buddhist, as the sister of the Dalai Lama, to have a rigorous Catholic education? Did the nuns expect you to forsake Buddhism for Catholicism?

PEMA. Oh well, the education, you know, I was sent to a convent school because these convent schools in India recognized to be the best schools for girls in India in those days. And then also, the nuns, they were very kind and, you know, they were really good educationalists. Most of the girls in the school were either, you know, Hindus or Muslims or Buddhists, and they were not really—I think about—only about 10 or 15 percent were Catholics.

The nuns were all—they, you know, understood our background and they didn't sort of really try to convert us. And for me, I already, you know, even at the age of 10, I already knew my own sort of roots and I was—I knew I was Buddhist and I don't think I could change my religion, even at that age.

GROSS. My guest is Jetsun Pema, the younger sister of the Dalai Lama. She's written a new autobiography. We'll talk more after a break.

This is FRESH AIR.

If you're just joining us, my guest is Jetsun Pema. She's the sister of the Dalai Lama and president of the Tibetan Children's Village, which oversees the resettlement and education of Tibetan children in exile. And she's written a new book called *Tibet: My Story.*

Your brother, the Dalai Lama, fled Tibet in 1959 and resettled in Dharamsala which has become the—kind of like Tibet in exile. Were you living in Dharamsala at the time?

PEMA. No, I was still, when in 1959, when His Holiness, you know, after the Tibetans had the uprising against the Chinese, he had to leave Tibet and seek asylum in India. And at that time, it was my—almost the final year of my schooling. So when he arrived, I was in school.

Then later, I joined him in Masouri (ph), in one of the hill stations where the Indian government had provided him with accommodation, and he was staying there. And in 1960, from Masouri, then he moved to Dharamsala. And in 1960 when I finished my school, then I went to Dharamsala and spent a couple of months there helping my sister with the work that she had—she was doing and looking after the Tibetan refugee children.

GROSS. Your sister died in 1964, and you took over her work . . .

PEMA. That's right.

GROSS. . . . overseeing the education and resettlement of Tibetan children living in exile in India. What was it like for you when you started doing this work—watching children refugees come to India, often with no parents, either because their parents were killed or because their parents had to stay behind?

PEMA. Yes, it was—in the beginning it was really very difficult situation for the children, as well as for those of—you know, like my sister and all those ladies who were looking after the children. It was then, in the beginning, they didn't have proper food, clothing, shelter—and everybody was coming. You know, the refugees were pouring into India from Tibet. And so many children were, you know, had skin infections and they had stomach ailments, and those earlier years of the refugees, it was really a terrible situation.

And many children lost their lives, and even many adults, you know, they lost their lives because they were not used to the climate in India. And also, they had to take long journeys across the mountainous regions to get into India. So, it was a very difficult time.

GROSS. What kind of schooling have you tried to give the children in India and how does it compare to the schooling that they would have received before the invasion in Tibet?

PEMA. Well, in—today in exile, 99 percent of Tibetan children receive education, and it's a modern education. They learn since now—since 1986, we have switched, you know, from English to Tibetan language as the medium of instruction up to the primary school level. Then from the—from primary school onwards, then the medium of instruction is in English.

And they get a very strong foundation in their own, you know, mother tongue, and then also their education is a education which is recognized by the Indian central board of secondary education, because unless we give our children an education which is recognized in the country, it would be very difficult for our children to pursue their further education in the various training centers and, you know, in the colleges and in the universities within India.

But then at the same time, what we are also emphasizing is

that His Holiness always says: "you must have a good education, but at the same time, in the end, you must be a good human being." So we want to give our children a value-oriented education so that these young people who finish their schools and go for further education and all, they should be good human beings and also good Tibetans.

GROSS. Some of the children have come to you as teenagers, and they have grown up in post-invasion Tibet. And I know you've had some trouble with these older teenagers who have come to Tibet. You write in your book that there has been some gang fighting and rock throwing. And it was very difficult to figure out how to deal with—with these problems.

Would you tell us a little bit about what you tried?

PEMA. Yes, this—you know, this special group of young people who are now coming in quite a large numbers, you know, escaping into exile, and these young people, most of them have never had any kind of formal education. And they have gone through a lot of hardship, and they've seen terrible things like they've seen their, you know, parents being sort of tortured in front of them; and they've seen their whole family disrupted because of the situation being what it is in Tibet.

And then—now when they came into exile, you know, they were not able to tackle with the freedom that we enjoy. You know, they couldn't believe that they could just get enough to eat every day and that, you know, they've got clothing. And you know, we try to look after them as best as we could.

But then at the same time, they had so much of anger and hatred in them. So you know, we felt that they were very aggressive and they were impolite. So we discussed together how we should look after these young people, and the first thing that was to make them feel that all of us, and also the school facilities and whatever we had, that it was for them; that we cared for them; that we wanted to look after them.

And you know, like sometimes they would play football or volleyball, and they would kick the balls. And one day, two or three, you know, footballs were going, and we always said: "it doesn't matter. Let them, you know, sort of bring out their anger on the balls and on the field playing and all."

And then later, it's surprising how they changed in a couple of months. Their whole attitude changed and the expressions on their face changed and it was just through letting them know that we cared for them.

GROSS. If you're just joining us, my guest is Jetsun Pema. She is the sister of the Dalai Lama and she's the president of the Tibetan Children's Village, which oversees the resettlement and education of Tibetan children in exile in India.

She's also written a new book called *Tibet: My Story.*

You write that ironically, exile has enabled the women of Tibet to evolve; to be liberated from the taboos which had previously confined them in Tibet. What are some of the taboos and restrictions that Tibetan women faced that you think they are getting out of now, living in exile?

PEMA. Well, in Tibet—in the old Tibet—Tibetan women didn't take any part in politics. And they didn't do any kind of, you know, like in the government service and all—you didn't see any kind of—any women. But then because of the occupation of Tibet by China and the brutality that the—you know, we saw over there. And I think the women, they really felt this very much, especially, you know, when they saw their sons and husbands being, you know, so ill-treated. And they, many of them, lost their, you know, sons and husbands.

Then, the Tibetan women, like when we had the uprising on the 10th of March, it was the women of Lhasa who were the ones who instigated, you know, all the people to come and, you know, try to protect His Holiness. And that's the time when the women really sort of stood up and they united, you know, together.

And then now in exile, Tibetan women, they get equal kind of education with the boys, and Tibetan women are now, you know, involved in politics and now today, like the Tibetan government, you know, we have a democratic system of government. They are members of the parliament in exile, they are selected, you know, they are voted by the people. And there are 46 members of parliament, and of that, 12 are women, which means more than—almost 35 percent are women.

So the Tibetan women are really coming forward and, you know, they are doing very well.

GROSS. I should point out that you are the minister of education.

PEMA. I was. Not anymore, no. I resigned.

GROSS. Former, OK.

PEMA. Yes, that's right.

GROSS. That's right.

PEMA. Yes.

GROSS. OK. And is your daughter elected to the parliament herself?

PEMA. Yes, yes. She's serving her second term.

GROSS. Mm-hmm.

PEMA. And yes, she's enjoying it.

GROSS. What do you miss most, geographically, about your country?

PEMA. Oh, I—the mountains and the lakes and the, you know, the clear blue sky, and the fresh air—unpolluted air. Yes.

GROSS. Describe what the mountains look like.

PEMA. The mountains?

GROSS. Yeah.

PEMA. Well, they look very, very high and, you know, magnificent and it's always—you always have these mountains which are snow-covered very high up. And then you have these kind of, you know, wonderful grassland with lots of the yak and the sheep and all. And then it's all green and you have a beautiful river, sort of flowing through this large stretch of green grassland. And then far away, you see the mountain peaks.

GROSS. Your brother the Dalai Lama sent you back to Tibet in 1980 on a kind of fact-finding mission to see what life was like there. And one of the things you discovered was your parents' old house was now an inn for Chinese military officers. That must have been quite startling.

PEMA. Yes, it was quite startling. But then, what was more startling is that, you know, you have—you see Lhasa. If you go up the Potala and you see—look down into the city, all you—you don't see anymore of the Tibetan houses. It's full of army, sort of barracks, and you have these horrible-looking sort of buildings, you know, four or five storeys high, with tin sheet roofs. And it's—it's terrible.

GROSS. I know you have a small part in the movie *Seven Years in Tibet,* and in fact you play the role of your mother, the Dalai Lama's mother.

PEMA. Yes.

GROSS. And the movie *Kundun,* which is about the young Dalai Lama—the movie made by Martin Scorcese that's opening later this year. Your daughter plays the role—one of your daughters plays the role of . . .

PEMA. Yes.

GROSS. . . . your mother.

PEMA. That's right.

GROSS. What did the Dalai Lama have to say about you and your daughter being involved in these movies?

PEMA. Oh well, he approved of it, you know, because we told him about these movies and he approved of that, yes. And also my children and my brothers, my other brothers, they all felt that they couldn't see our mother being portrayed by somebody else. So, they told myself and my daughter to, oh, go ahead and do play the role of, you know, our mother in the two movies.

GROSS. My guest is Jetsun Pema, the younger sister of the Dalai Lama. She's written a new autobiography. We'll talk more after a break.

This is FRESH AIR.

Finding and Replacing Text

User's Guide

Overview

WHEN you need to review or change text in your document, use the Find and Replace commands on the Edit menu. Use Find to quickly locate all occurrences of the text you specify. To change a certain word or phrase used throughout your document, use Replace to make all the changes quickly and accurately. With Find and Replace, you can also:

• Find all occurrences of a certain word, phrase, or sequence of characters.

• Find text that has a certain format such as bold. You can replace the text with different text and also change the formatting. For example, you can replace *Winmark Corporation* with **Winmark, Inc.**

• Find and replace special characters such as tabs, optional hyphens, and paragraph marks.

Finding and Replacing Text

When you use Find and Replace, you can have Word find text that makes up a whole word only or that has a certain pattern of capitalization. For example, you can find "and" but skip "candle" and "band" or find all occurrences of the name Green but skip the color green.

Word normally searches the main text of the document that is displayed on the screen. To include hidden text in the search, make sure the text is displayed. Select the Show Hidden Text check box, a View option in the Preferences dialog box (Tools menu) to display the text. To search in footnotes, headers, or footers you must first open the footnote, header, or footer window. Then place the insertion point in the window and choose Find or Replace.

To find text

Word searches for the specified text throughout the main text of the document unless you select the part of the document you want searched.

1 From the Edit menu, choose Find.

2 In the Find What box, type the text you're searching for.

If you used Find or Replace in your current work session, the text you last searched for is selected in the Find What box. Type over the text to search for different text.

You can type up to 255 characters in the Find What box. Text scrolls horizontally in the box as you type.

If text formats are listed below the Find What box, select Clear from the Format box. Otherwise, Word finds only occurrences of the text having the listed formats.

3 Select any options you want to control the search.

To do this	Select
Find only separate words, not the sequence of characters occurring in other words.	Match Whole Word Only
Find only words having a certain pattern of uppercase and lower-case letters.	Match Case
Change the proposed search direction or part of the document in which Word searches.	An option in the Search box

4 Choose the Find Next button to begin searching.

Word selects the first occurrence of the text and scrolls to it in the document so you can see the text in your document. To find the next occurrence of the text, choose the Find Next button again.

To edit the found text, click in the document. The Find dialog box remains open behind the document window. To continue the search after editing, click in the Find dialog box to make it active, or choose Find from the Edit menu again, and then choose the Find Next button.

If you began the search from the middle of the document, Word asks if you want to continue searching from the beginning (or end, depending on the search direction). Choose the Yes button to search the remainder of the document, or choose the No button to stop the search. When all text is searched, Word notifies you that it's reached the end of the document.

To replace text
Word replaces the specified text throughout the document unless you select a part of the document. If you're making

major changes, it's a good idea to save your document before you start the replace procedure. That way, if you don't like the results, you can close the document without saving the changes.

1 From the Edit menu, choose Replace.

2 In the Find What box, type the text you want to find and replace with different text.

If you used Find or Replace in your current work session, the text you last searched for is selected in the Find What box. Type over the text to search for different text.

If text formats are listed below the Find What box, select Clear from the Format box unless you want to find only occurrences of the text that have that formatting.

3 In the Replace With box, type the replacement text.

If you used Replace in your current work session, the replacement text you last specified is selected in the Replace With box. Type over the text to specify different replacement text.

You can type up to 255 characters in the Replace With box. Text scrolls horizontally in the box as you type.

If text formats are listed below the Replace With box, select Clear from the Format box unless you want to change the formatting of the found text.

4 Select any options you want to control the search.

To do this	Select
Replace only separate words, not the sequence of characters occurring in other words.	Match Whole Word Only
Replace only words having a certain pattern of uppercase and lowercase letters.	Match Case
Change the proposed search direction.	An option in the Search box

5 To begin searching, choose the Find Next or Replace All button.

To do this	Choose this button
Confirm each change. When Word finds an occurrence of the search text, choose the Replace button to change the text or choose the Find Next button to continue without changing this occurrence.	Find Next

Replace all occurrences of the   Replace All
search text without confirmation.
Word displays the number of
changes in the lower-left corner of
the window. If you selected a range
of text and Selection is the Search
option, Word makes changes only
in the selected part of the
document.

Note If you make many changes using the Replace command,
Word uses a considerable amount of memory. To free memory
so that Word can work more quickly, perform a normal save on
your document after using Replace. For instructions on saving
documents, see Chapter 2, "Opening, Saving, and Deleting Documents."

To cancel the Find or Replace command
• To cancel a search or replacement in progress, choose the
Cancel button in the dialog box, or press COMMAND+PERIOD or the
ESC key.

To delete text using Replace
It's a good idea to save your document before deleting text
with the Replace command. That way, if you delete the wrong
text, you can simply close the document without saving the
changes.

1 In the Find What box of the Replace dialog box, type the text
you want to find and delete.

2 Delete any text in the Replace With box.

3 If formats are shown below the Replace With box, select Clear
from the Format box.

If formats are specified, Word changes the format of the found
text instead of deleting it.

4 Choose the Find Next or Replace All button.

Using the Voice Mail System

The following are the instructions you will need to access the Voice Mail System for the first time.

1. DIAL YOUR ACCESS CODE

From your desk: x4600 - enter passcode (see #2)
Away from your desk: x2200 - * mailbox number then passcode

There will be a .23 cents per minute charge when accessing the system by the 800 number.

Remote access: 1-800-555-5555 / 201-555-5550
You will hear the company greeting. **Press *, mailbox number, then passcode.**

2. FIRST CALL: ENTER THE PASSCODE 1990. This is the setup passcode for first-time users. You will use it only on your **FIRST** call.

3. Follow instructions and complete the tutorial. You **MUST** complete all 3 steps.

> 1. Make your own passcode.
> 2. Make your personal greeting.
> 3. Say your name.

CONGRATULATIONS! YOU HAVE NOW SET UP YOUR VOICE MAILBOX.

NEED HELP? CALL - (201) 555-5500

TO CALL FORWARD YOUR PHONE TO VOICE MAIL:

Call forward all calls:	*-7-4600	Cancel: # 7
Call forward after 5 rings:	*-5-4600	Cancel: # 5
Call forward if busy:	*-8-4600	Cancel: # 8

MAILBOX LIMITS

Number of Messages:	25
Message Length:	4 minutes
Storage of Unplayed Messages:	10 days
Storage of Played Messages:	4 days

VOICE MAIL USER GUIDE

PLAYING YOUR MESSAGES

DIAL THE ACCESS CODE

> Refer to step # 1 on page # 1

Enter * and your mailbox number then passcode

The system will tell you the number of urgent and unplayed messages and the total number of messages.

Press P – Plays the first message
   While playing a message you may:

R – Review same message

A – Answer back to the person who sent the message. **NOTE:** If you press **A** and the system says "I cannot answer this message," it was not sent using the **M** key.

G – Give a message to another mailbox. Enter mailbox number (s) to give message to:
   Press # to record comments
      x to send comments and message

T – Travel to the top of the next message
K – Keeps message
D – Discards message
M – Make a new message – Enter mailbox number (s)
                # to record message
                x to send message

ADDITIONAL FEATURES WHILE PLAYING A MESSAGE

* - Rewind 5 seconds
# - Forward 5 seconds
1 - Pause 30 seconds

NOTE: You may press **K** or **D** at any time during a message. Then press **P** to play the next message. All messages are date and time stamped.

NOTE: The system will play receipts before messages. To stop the receipt press **K** or **D** then **P** to play message. Receipts DO NOT count as a message. Remember to listen for the words "That was your last UNPLAYED MESSAGE." This confirms you have heard all the new messages before playing the old ones.

Using the Voice Mail System

ALWAYS PRESS **X** to exit the system.

MAKE A MISTAKE? PAUSE and **LISTEN**—The system will **REPEAT** the responses.

MAKING MESSAGES FOR OTHER USERS

ALWAYS MAKE and **SEND** messages to other users from **YOUR** mailbox. (If you do not know the mailbox number, press 9* to dial by name.)

Access your mailbox.

Press **M**-Make message

Enter mailbox number (s). You can enter a combination of mailbox numbers and/or Distribution List numbers. If you enter a number and want to cancel it, press *. When you are ready to record a message, press #.

After making a message, you may:
R – Review message
A – Append to message
D – Delete message and start over

Press **x** – To send message
If you decide not to send the message, simply press **D** and **x** to cancel it and return to the main menu.

or

Press M for:

MESSAGE ADDRESSING OPTIONS

C – Confidential: Message cannot be passed to another mailbox.

R – Request receipt: Notifies you if the person has or has not played your message.

U – Urgent: Moves a message to the front of the cue. Urgent messages are played first. (This is a management-approved feature.)

X – Exit options

X – Send message

REMINDER – You must press **X TWICE** to send a message when you are using message options.

USER OPTIONS

These features allow a user to make changes to the mailbox. To access user options: Access your mailbox.

Press **U** – User options

G – Change greeting: This is the greeting that callers hear when they call your extension or mailbox.

N – Change name: Say your name. Your name is played when you send a message internally using the **M** key; it is also the name that is in the Voice Mail Directory.

P – Passcode: You may change your passcode as often as you like. It must be 4 numbers.

NOTE: When accessing your mailbox, if you enter the passcode incorrectly, you must enter the correct passcode **TWICE** before you can gain access to your mailbox.

T – Tutorial: Repeats the introductory tutorial.

L – Distribution list: See page 5.

Mel Allen: Profile of a Sportscaster

Scripps Howard News Service

(Jun 19, 1996—08:35 EST)—"Yogi Berra on first base. Mickey Mantle at bat with the count of one ball, no strikes. Left-handed pitcher Chuck Stobbs on the mound. Mickey Mantle, a switch-hitter batting right-handed, digs in at the plate. Here's the pitch . . . Mantle swings . . . There's a tremendous drive going into deep left field! It's going, going, and it's going over the bleachers and over the sign atop the bleachers into the yards of houses across the street! It's got to be one of the longest home runs I've ever seen hit! How about that!"

—Mel Allen, describing a "tape-measure" homer by the Yankees' Mickey Mantle, April 17, 1953, as quoted in Curt Smith's book *Voices of the Game*

For many of us growing up, Mel Allen was baseball.

He was such an essential part of the game for so many years—he was the only announcer to broadcast games in seven decades—that it seemed the World Series couldn't be played without Allen behind the microphone.

Surely there were fans away from New York City who thought all Allen did was broadcast the World Series every year, usually with Red Barber. In truth, the reason Allen did so many Series—20 in all—was because he was the principal broadcaster for the New York Yankees and the Yankees were almost always in the World Series back in those days, as were Barber's Brooklyn Dodgers.

When Allen died Sunday at 83, many of us thought the game had lost its finest announcer.

"Broadcasting is so subjective; what is chocolate for one person is vanilla for another," Curt Smith, author of *Voices of the Game,* said Monday from Wisconsin. "But in my way of thinking, yes, Mel Allen was the best baseball broadcaster we've ever had.

"It was as if a florist decorated his voice. He could do more with his voice than any other broadcaster. In the 1950's, *Variety* came out with a poll showing that Mel Allen's voice was one of the 25 most recognizable voices in the world—and he was the only broadcaster on the list."

Allen was born Melvin Allen Israel to Russian immigrants, Feb. 14, 1913, in Johns, Ala. He attended the University of Alabama, earning a law degree, but wound up broadcasting Alabama football games for $5 per game. After passing his bar exam in 1936, he went to New York for a brief vacation and decided "for a lark" to audition at CBS Radio. He won out over 60 applicants, became a staff announcer and then joined the Yankees in 1940.

Except for four years in the Army, Allen held that post until 1964. In addition to his 20 Series, Allen did 24 All-Star Games, 14 Rose Bowls, five Orange Bowls and two Sugar Bowls—not to mention a weekly network program and newsreels.

Baseball, of course, is what he is remembered for most, swirling his drawling Alabamanisms into his delivery. From his opening line ("Hello there, everybody, this is Mel Allen") to his play-by-play ("Three-and-two, what'll he do?"), his trademark line ("How about that!") and his commercials (home runs sometimes became "Ballantine blasts" to honor a beer company or "White Owl wallops" for a cigar maker), every line was pure Allen.

"It was the tenor, the resonance," said Smith. "Red Barber would report a game, Mel Allen would become involved, with his voice booming to the listener. Barber was white wine, crepes suzette and bluegrass music; Allen was beer, hot dogs and the United States Marine Band."

Allen was seen as a Yankee through and through, especially by Yankee haters, and there were times he lived up to that billing. When New York's Bill Bevens pitched a World Series no-hitter for 8 2/3 innings in 1947, Allen didn't mention it on the air lest he jinx it.

"Obviously what I said or didn't say in the booth wasn't going to influence anything that happened on the field," Allen said to Smith in *Voices of the Game*. "But I've always known that players on the bench don't mention a no-hitter; they respect the dugout tradition. And I've always done the same. It's part of the romance of the game; it's one of the great things that separates it from the other sports, like the seventh-inning stretch or 'Take Me Out to the Ball Game.' Or the biggest difference of all in a World Series or any other baseball—the lack of a clock."

Barber took over later in the game and mentioned the no-hitter, which the Dodgers broke up and won in the ninth inning.

Generally, however, Allen played it straight during Yankee World Series broadcasts. In fact, in 1953, when the Dodgers' Carl Furillo homered in the ninth inning to tie the last game, Allen was so excited with his call that fans flooded the Yankee Stadium switchboard with complaints.

Strangely, in 1963, when the Los Angeles Dodgers swept the Yankees in four straight World Series games, Allen was stricken with a sudden attack of laryngitis during Game 4. The Dodgers' Vin Scully had to fill in for him. Allen said it was from a recurring nasal condition, but the Yankees fired him before the next season. No reason was ever given.

"The thought was that Ballantine was struggling and that they thought Allen was making too much money," Smith said. "There were all sorts of terrible rumors, none of which was true."

Allen was virtually blackballed until 1976 when he rejoined the Yankees on a part-time basis. Two years later, he and Barber were inducted into the Baseball Hall of Fame in Cooperstown, N.Y.

But Allen truly achieved his renaissance in '77, when he became the host for "This Week in Baseball." On "TWIB" he chronicled the latest happenings in the game, while serving as a wonderful reminder of its past.

"'This Week in Baseball' was really his Damascus Road," Smith noted, "and it really turned into a second career for him. He was the voice of baseball for the next 20 years for a whole new generation of fans, just as I and many others learned about the game from his broadcasts of the Yankees and the World Series."

In every situation, Allen was as down home and friendly off the air as he was on the air, according to those who knew him.

"We became very good friends, and he was an extremely decent person and was always very kind and caring toward sportswriters and sportscasters who would come to him," Smith said. "That's what I want to remember about him."

How about that.

The First Appendectomy

William A. Nolen

THE patient, or better, victim, of my first major surgical venture was a man I'll call Mr. Polansky. He was fat, he weighed one hundred and ninety pounds and was five feet eight inches tall. He spoke only broken English. He had had a sore abdomen with all the classical signs and symptoms of appendicitis for twenty-four hours before he came to Bellevue.

After two months of my internship, though I had yet to do anything that could be decently called an "operation," I had had what I thought was a fair amount of operating time. I'd watched the assistant residents work, I'd tied knots, cut sutures and even, in order to remove a skin lesion, made an occasional incision. Frankly, I didn't think that surgery was going to be too damn difficult. I figured I was ready, and I was chomping at the bit to go, so when Mr. Polansky arrived I greeted him like a long-lost friend. He was overwhelmed at the interest I showed in his case. He probably couldn't understand why any doctor should be so fascinated by a case of appendicitis; wasn't it a common disease? It was just as well that he didn't realize my interest in him was so personal. He might have been frightened, and with good reason.

At any rate, I set some sort of record in preparing Mr. Polansky for surgery. He had arrived on the ward at four o'clock. By six I had examined him, checked his blood and urine, taken his chest x-ray and had him ready for the operating room.

George Walters, the senior resident on call that night, was to "assist" me during the operation. George was older than the rest of us. I was twenty-five at this time and he was thirty-two. He had taken his surgical training in Europe and was spending one year as a senior resident in an American hospital to establish eligibility for the American College of Surgeons. He had had more experience than the other residents and it took a lot to disturb his equanimity in the operating room. As it turned out, this made him the ideal assistant for me.

It was ten o'clock when we wheeled Mr. Polansky to the operating room. At Bellevue, at night, only two operating rooms were kept open—there were six or more going all day—so we had to

48

wait our turn. In the time I had to myself before the operation I had reread the section on appendectomy in the *Atlas of Operative Technique* in our surgical library, and had spent half an hour tying knots on the bedpost in my room. I was, I felt, "ready."

I delivered Mr. Polansky to the operating room and started an intravenous going in his arm. Then I left him to the care of the anesthetist. I had ordered a sedative prior to surgery, so Mr. Polansky was drowsy. The anesthetist, after checking his chart, soon had him sleeping.

Once he was asleep I scrubbed the enormous expanse of Mr. Polansky's abdomen for ten minutes. Then, while George placed the sterile drapes, I scrubbed my own hands for another five, mentally reviewing each step of the operation as I did so. Donning gown and gloves I took my place on the right side of the operating-room table. The nurse handed me the scalpel. I was ready to begin.

Suddenly my entire attitude changed. A split second earlier I had been supremely confident; now, with the knife finally in my hand, I stared down at Mr. Polansky's abdomen and for the life of me could not decide where to make the incision. The "landmarks" had disappeared. There was too much belly.

George waited a few seconds, then looked up at me and said, "Go ahead."

"What?" I asked.

"Make the incision," said George.

"Where?" I asked.

"Where?"

"Yes," I answered, "where?"

"Why, here, of course," said George and drew an imaginary line on the abdomen with his fingers.

I took the scalpel and followed where he had directed. I barely scratched Mr. Polansky.

"Press a little harder," George directed. I did. The blade went through the skin to a depth of perhaps one sixteenth of an inch.

"Deeper," said George.

There are five layers of tissue in the abdominal wall: skin, fat, fascia (a tough membranous tissue), muscle and peritoneum (the smooth, glistening, transparent inner lining of the abdomen). I cut down into the fat. Another sixteenth of an inch.

"Bill," said George, looking up at me, "this patient is big. There's at least three inches of fat to get through before we even reach the fascia. At the rate you're going, we won't be into the abdomen for another four hours. For God's sake, will you cut?"

I made up my mind not to be hesitant. I pressed down hard on the knife, and suddenly we were not only through the fat but through the fascia as well.

"Not that hard," George shouted, grabbing my right wrist with his left hand while with his other hand he plunged a gauze pack into the wound to stop the bleeding. "Start clamping," he told me.

The nurse handed us hemostats and we applied them to the numerous vessels I had so hastily opened. "All right," George said, "start tying."

I took the ligature material from the nurse and began to tie off the vessels. Or rather, I tried to tie off the vessels, because suddenly my knot-tying proficiency had melted away. The casual dexterity I had displayed on the bedpost a short hour ago was nowhere in evidence. My fingers, greasy with fat, simply would not perform. My ties slipped off the vessels, the sutures snapped in my fingers, at one point I even managed to tie the end of my rubber glove into the wound. It was, to put it bluntly, a performance in fumbling that would have made Robert Benchley blush.

Here I must give my first paean of praise to George. His patience during the entire performance was nothing short of miraculous. The temptation to pick up the catgut and do the tying himself must have been strong. He could have tied off all the vessels in two minutes. It took me twenty.

Finally we were ready to proceed. "Now," George directed, "split the muscle. But gently, please."

I reverted to my earlier tack. Fiber by fiber I spread the muscle which was the last layer but one that kept us from the inside of the abdomen. Each time I separated the fibers and withdrew my clamp, the fibers rolled together again. After five minutes I was no nearer the appendix than I had been at the start.

George could stand it no longer. But he was apparently afraid to suggest I take a more aggressive approach, fearing I would stick the clamp into, or possibly through, the entire abdomen. Instead he suggested that he help me by spreading the muscle in one direction while I spread it in the other. I made my usual infinitesimal attack on the muscle. In one fell swoop George spread the rest.

"Very well done," he complimented me. "Now let's get in."

We each took a clamp and picked up the tissue-paper-thin peritoneum. After two or three hesitant attacks with the scalpel I finally opened it. We were in the abdomen.

"Now," said George, "put your fingers in, feel the cecum [the portion of the bowel to which the appendix is attached] and bring it into the wound."

I stuck my right hand into the abdomen. I felt around—but what was I feeling? I had no idea.

It had always looked so simple when the senior resident did it. Open the abdomen, reach inside, pull up the appendix. Nothing to it. But apparently there was.

Everything felt the same to me. The small intestine, the large intestine, the cecum—how did one tell them apart without seeing them? I grabbed something and pulled it into the wound. Small intestine. No good. Put it back. I grabbed again. This time it was the sigmoid colon. Put it back. On my third try I had the small intestine again.

"The appendix must be in an abnormal position," I said to George. "I can't seem to find it."

"Mind if I try?" he asked.

"Not at all," I answered. "I wish you would."

Two of his fingers disappeared into the wound. Five seconds later they emerged, cecum between them, with the appendix flopping from it.

"Stuck down a little," he said kindly. "That's probably why you didn't feel it. It's a hot one," he added. "Let's get at it."

The nurse handed me the hemostats, and one by one I applied them to the mesentery of the appendix—the veil of tissue in which the blood vessels run. With George holding the veil between his fingers I had no trouble; I took the ligatures and tied the vessels without a single error. My confidence was coming back.

"Now," George directed, "put in your purse string." (The cecum is a portion of the bowel which has the shape of half a hemisphere. The appendix projects from its surface like a finger. In an appendectomy the routine procedure is to tie the appendix at its base and cut it off a little beyond the tie. Then the remaining stump is inverted into the cecum and kept there by tying the purse-string stitch. This was the stitch I was now going to sew.)

It went horribly. The wall of the cecum is not very thick—perhaps one eighth of an inch. The suture must be placed deeply enough in the wall so that it won't cut through when tied, but not so deep as to pass all the way through the wall. My sutures were alternately too superficial or too deep, but eventually I got the job done.

"All right," said George, "let's get the appendix out of here. Tie off the base."

I did.

"Now cut off the appendix."

At least in this, the definitive act of the operation, I would be decisive. I took the knife and with one quick slash cut through the appendix—too close to the ligature.

"Oh oh, watch it," said George. "That tie is going to slip."

It did. The appendiceal stump lay there, open. I felt faint.

"Don't panic," said George. "We've still got the purse string. I'll push the stump in—you pull up the stitch and tie. That will take care of it."

I picked up the two ends of the suture and put in the first stitch. George shoved the open stump into the cecum. It disappeared as I snugged my tie. Beautiful.

"Two more knots," said George. "Just to be safe."

I tied the first knot and breathed a sigh of relief. The appendiceal stump remained out of sight. On the third knot—for the sake of security—I pulled a little tighter. The stitch broke; the open stump popped up; the cecum disappeared into the abdomen. I broke out in a cold sweat and my knees started to crumble.

Even George momentarily lost his composure. "Bill," he said, grasping desperately for the bowel, "what did you have to do that for?" The low point of the operation had been reached.

By the time we had retrieved the cecum, Mr. Polansky's peritoneal cavity had been contaminated. My self-confidence was shattered. And still George let me continue. True, he all but held my hand as we retied and resutured, but the instruments were in my hand.

The closure was anticlimactic. Once I had the peritoneum sutured, things went reasonably smoothly. Two hours after we began, the operation was over. "Nice job," George said, doing his best to sound sincere.

"Thanks," I answered, lamely.

The scrub nurse laughed.

Mr. Polansky recovered, I am happy to report, though not without a long and complicated convalescence. His bowel refused to function normally for two weeks and he became enormously distended. He was referred to at our nightly conferences as "Dr. Nolen's pregnant man." Each time the reference was made, it elicited a shudder from me.

During his convalescence I spent every spare moment I could at Mr. Polansky's bedside. My feelings of guilt and responsibility were overwhelming. If he had died I think I would have given up surgery for good.

Life Stories

Michael Dorris

IN most cultures, adulthood is equated with self-reliance and responsibility, yet often Americans do not achieve this status until we are in our late twenties or early thirties—virtually the entire average lifespan of a person in a traditional non-Western society. We tend to treat prolonged adolescence as a warm-up for real life, as a wobbly ladder between childhood and legal maturity. Whereas a nineteenth-century Cheyenne or Lakota teenager was expected to alter self-conception in a split-second vision, we often meander through an analogous rite of passage for more than a decade—through high school, college, graduate school.

Though he had never before traveled alone outside his village, the Plains Indian male was expected at puberty to venture solo into the wilderness. There he had to fend for and sustain himself while avoiding the menace of unknown dangers, and there he had absolutely to remain until something happened that would transform him. Every human being, these tribes believed, was entitled to at least one moment of personal, enabling insight.

Anthropology proposes feasible psychological explanations for why this flash was eventually triggered: fear, fatigue, reliance on strange foods, the anguish of loneliness, stress, and the expectation of ultimate success all contributed to a state of receptivity. Every sense was quickened, alerted to perceive deep meaning, until at last the interpretation of an unusual event—a dream, a chance encounter, or an unexpected vista—reverberated with significance. Through this unique prism, abstractly preserved in a vivid memory or song, a boy caught foresight of both his adult persona and his vocation, the two inextricably entwined.

The best approximations that many of us get to such a heady sense of eventuality come in the performance of the jobs we hold during summer vacation. Summers are intermissions, and once we hit our teens it is during these breaks in our structured regimen that we initially taste the satisfaction of remuneration that is earned, not merely doled. Tasks defined as work are not graded, they are compensated; they have a worth that is inarguable because it translates into hard currency. Wage labor—

and in the beginning, this generally means a confining, repetitive chore for which we are quickly overqualified—paradoxically brings a sense of blooming freedom. At the outset, the complaint to a peer that business supersedes fun is oddly liberating—no matter what drudgery requires your attention, it is by its very required nature serious and adult.

At least that's how it seemed to me. I come from a line of people hard hit by the Great Depression. My mother and her sisters went to work early in their teens—my mother operated a kind of calculator known as a comptometer while her sisters spent their days, respectively, at a peanut factory and at Western Union. My grandmother did piecework sewing. Their efforts, and the Democratic Party, saw them through, and to this day they never look back without appreciation for their later solvency. They take nothing for granted. Accomplishments are celebrated, possessions are valuable, in direct proportion to the labor entailed to acquire them; anything easily won or bought on credit is suspect. When I was growing up we were far from wealthy, but what money we had was correlated to the hours one of us had logged. My eagerness to contribute to, or at least not diminish, the coffer was countered by the arguments of those whose salaries kept me in school: my higher education was a sound group investment. The whole family was adamant that I have the opportunities they had missed and, no matter how much I objected, they stinted themselves to provide for me.

Summer jobs were therefore a relief, an opportunity to pull a share of the load. As soon as the days turned warm I began to peruse the classifieds, and when the spring semester was done, I was ready to punch a clock. It even felt right. Work in June, July, and August had an almost biblical aspect: in the hot, canicular weather your brow sweats, just as God had ordained. Moreover, summer jobs had the luxury of being temporary. No matter how onerous, how off my supposed track, employment terminated with the falling leaves and I was back to real life. So, during each annual three-month leave from secondary school and later from the university, I compiled an eclectic resumé: lawn cutter, hair sweeper in a barber shop, lifeguard, delivery boy, mail carrier, file clerk, youth program coordinator on my Montana reservation, ballroom dance instructor, theater party promoter, night-shift hospital records keeper, human adding machine in a Paris bank, encyclopedia salesman, newspaper stringer, recreation bus manager, salmon fisherman.

The summer I was eighteen a possibility arose for a rotation at the post office, and I grabbed it. There was something casually sophisticated about work that required a uniform, about having a federal ranking, even if it was GS-1 (Temp/Sub), and it was flattering to be entrusted with a leather bag containing who knew what important correspondence. Every day I was assigned a new beat, usually in a rough neighborhood avoided whenever possible by regular carriers, and I proved quite capable of complicating what would normally be fairly routine missions. The low point came on the first of August when I diligently delivered four blocks' worth of welfare checks to the right numbers on the wrong streets. It is no fun to snatch unexpected wealth from the hands of those who have but moments previously opened their mailboxes and received a bonus.

After my first year of college, I lived with relatives on an Indian reservation in eastern Montana and filled the only post available: Coordinator of Youth Programs. I was seduced by the language of the announcement into assuming that there existed Youth Programs to be coordinated. In fact, the Youth consisted of a dozen bored, disgruntled kids—most of them my cousins—who had nothing better to do each day than to show up at what was euphemistically called "the gym" and hate whatever Program I had planned for them. The Youth ranged in age from fifteen to five and seemed to have as their sole common ambition the determination to smoke cigarettes. This put them at immediate and ongoing odds with the Coordinator, who on his first day naively encouraged them to sing the "Doe, a deer, a female deer" song from *The Sound of Music.* They looked at me, that bleak morning, and I looked at them, each boy and girl equipped with a Pall Mall behind an ear, and we all knew we faced a long, struggle-charged battle. It was to be a contest of wills, the hearty and wholesome versus prohibited vice. I stood for dodge ball, for collecting bugs in glass jars, for arts and crafts; they had pledged a preternatural allegiance to sloth. The odds were not in my favor and each waking dawn I experienced the lightheadedness of anticipated exhaustion, that thrill of giddy dissociation in which nothing seems real or of great significance. Finally, I went with the flow and learned to inhale.

The next summer, I decided to find work in an urban setting for a change, and was hired as a general office assistant in the Elsa Hoppenfeld Theatre Party Agency, located above Sardi's restaurant in New York City. The agency consisted of Elsa Hoppenfeld herself, Rita Frank, her regular deputy, and me. Elsa was a gregarious Viennese woman who established contacts through honesty, hard work, and personal charm, and she spent much of the time away from the building courting trade. Rita was therefore both my immediate supervisor and constant companion; she had the most incredible fingernails I had ever seen— long, carefully shaped pegs lacquered in cruel primary colors and hard as stone—and an attitude about her that could only be described as zeal.

The goal of a theater party agent is to sell blocks of tickets to imminent Broadway productions, and the likely buyers are charities, B'nai B'riths, Hadassahs, and assorted other fund-raising organizations. We received commissions on volume, and so it was necessary to convince a prospect that a play—preferably an expensive musical—for which we had reserved the rights to seats would be a boffo smash hit.

The object of our greatest expectation that season was an extravaganza called *Chu Chem,* a saga that aspired to ride the coattails of *Fiddler on the Roof* into entertainment history. It starred the estimable Molly Picon and told the story of a family who had centuries ago gone from Israel to China during the Diaspora, yet had, despite isolation in an alien environment, retained orthodox culture and habits. The crux of the plot revolved around a man with several marriageable daughters and nary a kosher suitor within five thousand miles. For three months Rita and I waxed eloquent in singing the show's praises. We sat in our little office, behind facing desks, and every noon while she redid her nails I ordered out from a deli that offered such exotic (to me) delicacies as fried egg sandwiches, lox and cream cheese, pastrami, tongue. I developed of necessity and habit a telephone voice laced with a distinctly Yiddish accent. It could have been a great career. However, come November, *Chu Chem* bombed. Its closing was such a financial catastrophe for all concerned that when the following January one Monsieur Dupont advertised on the placement board at my college, I decided to put an ocean between me and my former trusting clientele.

M. Dupont came to campus with the stated purpose of interviewing candidates for teller positions in a French bank. Successful applicants, required to be fluent *en français,* would be rewarded with three well-paid months and a rent-free apartment in Paris. On my way to the language lab, I registered for an appointment.

57

The only French in the interview was *Bonjour, ça va?*, after which M. Dupont switched into English and described the wonderful deal on charter air flights that would be available to those who got the nod. Round-trip to Amsterdam, via Reykjavík, leaving the day after exams and returning in mid-September, no changes or substitutions. I signed up on the spot. I was to be a *banquier*, with a *pied-à-terre* in Montparnasse!

Unfortunately, when I arrived with only $50 in traveler's checks in my pocket—the flight had cleaned me out, but who needed money since my paycheck started right away—no one in Paris had ever heard of M. Dupont. *Alors.*

I stood in the Gare du Nord and considered my options. There weren't any. I scanned a listing of Paris hotels and headed for the cheapest one: the Hotel Villedo, $10 a night. The place had an ambiance that I persuaded myself was antique, despite the red light above the sign. The only accommodation available was "the bridal suite," a steal at $20. The glass door to my room didn't lock and in the adjacent room there was a rather continual floor show, but at some point I must have dozed off. When I awoke the church bells were ringing, the sky was pink, and I felt renewed. No little setback was going to spoil my adventure. I stretched, then walked to a mirror that hung above the sink next to the bed. I leaned forward to punctuate my resolve with a confident look in the eye.

The sink disengaged and fell to the floor. Water gushed. In panic I rummaged through my open suitcase, stuffed two pairs of underpants into the pipe to quell the flow, and before the dam broke, I was out the door. I barreled through the lobby of the first bank I passed, asked to see the director, and told the startled man my sad story. For some reason, whether from shock or pity, he hired me at $1.27 an hour to be a cross-checker of foreign currency transactions, and with two phone calls found me lodgings at a commercial school's dormitory.

From 8 to 5 each weekday my duty was to sit in a windowless room with six impeccably dressed people, all of whom were totaling identical additions and subtractions. We were highly dignified with each other, very professional, no *tutoyering*. Monsieur Saint presided, but the formidable Mademoiselle was the true power; she oversaw each of our columns and shook her head sadly at my American-shaped numbers.

My legacy from that summer, however, was more than an enduring penchant for crossed 7s. After I had worked for six weeks, M. Saint asked me during a coffee break why I didn't follow the example of other foreign students he had known and depart the office at noon in order to spend the afternoon touring the sights of Paris with the Alliance Française.

"Because," I replied in my halting French, "that costs money. I depend upon my full salary the same as any of you." M. Saint nodded gravely and said no more, but then on the next Friday he presented me with a white envelope along with my check.

"Do not open this until you have left the Société Général," he said ominously. I thought I was fired for the time I had mixed up kroner and guilders, and, once on the sidewalk, I steeled myself to read the worst. I felt the quiet panic of blankness.

"Dear Sir," I translated the perfectly formed script. "You are a person of value. It is not correct that you should be in our beautiful city and not see it. Therefore we have amassed a modest sum to pay the tuition for a two-week afternoon program for you at the Alliance Française. Your wages will not suffer, for it is your assignment to appear each morning in this bureau and reacquaint us with the places you have visited. We shall see them afresh through your eyes." The letter had thirty signatures, from the director to the janitor, and stuffed inside the envelope was a sheaf of franc notes in various denominations.

I rushed back to the tiny office. M. Saint and Mademoiselle had waited, and accepted my gratitude with their usual controlled smiles and precise handshakes. But they had blown their Gallic cover, and for the next ten days and then through all the weeks until I went home in September, our branch was awash with sightseeing paraphernalia. Everyone had advice, favorite haunts, criticisms of the Alliance's choices or explanations. Paris passed through the bank's granite walls as sweetly as a June breeze through a window screen, and ever afterward the lilt of overheard French, a photograph of Sacre-Coeur or the Louvre, even a monthly bank statement, recalls to me that best of all summers.

I didn't wind up in an occupation with any obvious connection to the careers I sampled during my school breaks, but I never altogether abandoned those brief professions either. They were jobs not so much to be held as to be weighed, absorbed, and incorporated, and, collectively, they carried me forward into adult life like an escalator, unfolding a particular pattern at once amazing and inevitable.

First Job

Maya Angelou

MY room had all the cheeriness of a dungeon and the appeal of a tomb. It was going to be impossible to stay there, but leaving held no attraction for me, either. The answer came to me with the suddenness of a collision. I would go to work. Mother wouldn't be difficult to convince; after all, in school I was a year ahead of my grade and Mother was a firm believer in self-sufficiency. In fact, she'd be pleased to think that I had that much gumption, that much of her in my character. (She liked to speak of herself as the original "do-it-yourself" girl.)

Once I had settled on getting a job, all that remained was to decide which kind of job I was most fitted for. My intellectual pride had kept me from selecting typing, shorthand or filing as subjects in school, so office work was ruled out. War plants and shipyards demanded birth certificates, and mine would reveal me to be fifteen, and ineligible for work. So the well-paying defense jobs were also out. Women had replaced men on the streetcars as conductors and motormen, and the thought of sailing up and down the hills of San Francisco in a dark-blue uniform, with a money changer at my belt, caught my fancy.

Mother was as easy as I had anticipated. The world was moving so fast, so much money was being made, so many people were dying in Guam, and Germany, that hordes of strangers became good friends overnight. How could she have the time to think about my academic career?

To her question of what I planned to do, I replied that I would get a job on the streetcars. She rejected the proposal with, "They don't accept black people on the streetcars."

I would like to claim an immediate fury that was followed by the noble determination to break the restricting tradition. But the truth is, my first reaction was one of disappointment. I'd pictured myself, dressed in a neat blue serge suit, my money changer swinging jauntily at my waist, and a cheery smile for the passengers that would make their own work day brighter.

From disappointment, I gradually ascended the emotional ladder to haughty indignation, and finally to that state of stubbornness where the mind is locked like the jaws of an enraged bulldog.

I would go to work on the streetcars and wear a blue serge suit. Mother gave me her support with one of her usual terse asides, "That's what you want to do? Then nothing beats a *trial* but a failure. Give it everything you've got. I've told you many times, 'Can't Do is like Don't Care,' Neither of them has a home."

Translated, that meant there is nothing a person can't do, and there should be nothing a human being doesn't care about. It was the most positive encouragement I could have hoped for.

In the offices of the Market Street Railway Company, the receptionist seemed as surprised to see me there as I was surprised to find the interior dingy and drab. Somehow I had expected waxed surfaces and carpeted floors. If I had met no resistance. I might have decided against working for such a poor-mouth-looking concern. As it was, I explained that I had come to see about a job. She asked, was I sent by an agency, and when I replied that I was not, she told me they were only accepting applicants from agencies.

The classified pages of the morning papers had listed advertisements for motorettes and conductorettes, and I reminded her of that. She gave me a face full of astonishment that my suspicious nature would not accept.

"I am applying for the job listed in this morning's *Chronicle*, and I'd like to be presented to your personnel manager." While I spoke in supercilious accents, and looked at the room as if I had an oil well in my own backyard, my armpits were being pricked by millions of hot pointed needles. She saw her escape and dived into it.

"He's out. He's out for the day. You might call him tomorrow, and if he's in, I'm sure you can see him." Then she swiveled her chair around on its rusty screws, and with that I was supposed to be dismissed.

"May I ask his name?"

She half turned, acting surprised to find me still there.

"His name? Whose name?"

"Your personnel manager."

We were firmly joined in the hypocrisy to play out the scene.

"The personnel manager? Oh, he's Mr. Cooper, but I'm not sure you'll find him here tomorrow. He's . . . . Oh, but you can try."

"Thank you."

"You're welcome."

And I was out of the musty room and into the even mustier lobby. In the street I saw the receptionist and myself going faithfully through paces that were stale with familiarity, although I had never encountered that kind of situation before and, probably, neither had she. We were like actors who, knowing the play by heart, were still able to cry afresh over the old tragedies and laugh spontaneously at the comic situations.

The miserable little encounter had nothing to do with me, the me of me, any more that it had to do with that silly clerk. The incident was a recurring dream concocted years before by whites, and it eternally came back to haunt us all. The secretary and I were like people in a scene where, because of harm done by one ancestor to another, we were bound to duel to the death. Also, because the play must end somewhere.

I went further than forgiving the clerk; I accepted her as a fellow victim of the same puppeteer.

On the streetcar, I put my fare into the box, and the conductorette looked at me with the usual hard eyes of white contempt. "Move into the car, please move on in the car." She patted her money changer.

Her Southern nasal accent sliced my meditation, and I looked deep into my thoughts. All lies, all comfortable lies. The receptionist was not innocent and neither was I. The whole charade we had played out in that waiting room had directly to do with me, black, and her, white.

I wouldn't move into the streetcar but stood on the ledge over the conductor, glaring. My mind shouted so energetically that the announcement made my veins stand out, and my mouth tighten into a prune.

I WOULD HAVE THE JOB. I WOULD BE A CONDUCTORETTE AND SLING A FULL MONEY CHANGER FROM MY BELT. I WOULD.

The next three weeks were a honeycomb of determination with apertures for the days to go in and out. The black organizations to whom I appealed for support bounced me back and forth like a shuttlecock on a badminton court. Why did I insist on that particular job? Openings were going begging that paid nearly twice the money. The minor officials with whom I was able to win an audience thought me mad. Possibly I was.

Downtown San Francisco became alien and cold, and the streets I had loved in a personal familiarity were unknown lanes that twisted with malicious intent. My trips to the streetcar office were of the frequency of a person on salary. The struggle expanded. I was no longer in conflict only with the Market Street Railway but with the marble lobby of the building that housed its offices, and elevators and their operators.

During this period of strain, Mother and I began our first steps on the long path toward mutual adult admiration. She never asked for reports and I didn't offer any details. But every morning she made breakfast, gave me carfare and lunch money, as if I were going to work. She comprehended that in the struggle lies the joy. That I was no glory seeker was obvious to her, and that I had to exhaust every possibility before giving in was also clear.

On my way out of the house one morning she said, "Life is going to give you just what you put in it. Put your whole heart in everything you do, and pray; then you can wait." Another time she reminded me that, "God helps those who help themselves." She had a store of aphorisms that she dished out as the occasion demanded. Strangely, as bored as I was with her clichés, her inflection gave them something new, and set me thinking for a little while at least. Later, when asked how I got my job, I was never able to say exactly. I only knew that one day, which was tiresomely like all the others before it, I sat in the Railway office, waiting to be interviewed. The receptionist called me to her desk and shuffled a bundle of papers to me. They were job application forms. She said they had to be filled in triplicate. I had little time to wonder if I had won or not, for the standard questions reminded me of the necessity for lying. How old was I? List my previous jobs, starting from the last held and go backward to the first. How much money did I earn, and why did I leave the position? Give two references (not relatives). I kept my face blank (an old art) and wrote quickly the fable of Marguerite Johnson, aged nineteen, former companion and driver for Mrs. Annie Henderson (a White Lady) in Stamps, Arkansas.

I was given blood tests, aptitude tests, and physical coordination tests; then, on a blissful day, I was hired as the first black on the San Francisco streetcars.

Mother gave me the money to have my blue serge suit tailored, and I learned to fill out work cards, operate the money changer and punch transfers. The time crowded together, and at an End of Days I was swinging on the back of the rackety trolley, smiling sweetly and persuading my charges to "step forward in the car, please."

For one whole semester the streetcars and I shimmied up and scooted down the sheer hills of San Francisco. I lost some of my need for the black ghetto's shielding-sponge quality, as I clanged and cleared my way down Market Street, with its honky-tonk homes for homeless sailors, past the quiet retreat of Golden Gate Park, and along closed undwelled-in-looking dwellings of the Sunset District.

My workshifts were split so haphazardly that it was easy to believe that my superiors had chosen them maliciously. Upon mentioning my suspicions to Mother, she said, "Don't you worry about it. You ask for what you want, and you pay for what you get. And I'm going to show you that it ain't no trouble when you pack double."

She stayed awake to drive me out to the car barn at four-thirty in the mornings, or to pick me up when I was relieved just before dawn. Her awareness of life's perils convinced her that while I would be safe on the public conveyances, she "wasn't about to trust a taxi driver with her baby."

When the spring classes began, I resumed my commitment with formal education. I was so much wiser and older, so much more independent, with a bank account and clothes that I had bought for myself, that I was sure I had learned and earned the magic formula that would make me a part of the life my contemporaries led.

Not a bit of it. Within weeks, I realized that my schoolmates and I were on paths moving away from each other. They were concerned and excited over the approaching football games. They concentrated great interest on who was worthy of being student body president, and when the metal bands would be removed from their teeth, while I remembered conducting a streetcar in the uneven hours of the morning.

Nick Salerno

Studs Terkel

HE has been driving a city garbage truck for eighteen years. He is forty-one, married, has three daughters. He works a forty-hour, five-day week, with occasional overtime. He has a crew of three laborers. "I usually get up at five-fifteen. I get to the city parking lot, you check the oil, your water level, then proceed for the ward yard. I meet the men, we pick up our work sheet." You get just like the milkman's horse, you get used to it. If you remember the milkman's horse, all he had to do was whistle and whooshhh! That's it. He knew just where to stop, didn't he? You pull up until you finish the alley. Usually thirty homes on each side. You have thirty stops in an alley. I have nineteen alleys a week. They're called units. Sometimes I can't finish 'em, that's how heavy they are, this bein' an old neighborhood. I'll sit there until they pick up this one stop. You got different thoughts. Maybe you got a problem at home. Maybe one of the children aren't feeling too good. Like my second one, she's a problem with homework. Am I doin' the right thing with her? Pressing her a little bit with math. Or you'll read the paper. You always daydream.

Some stops, there's one can, they'll throw that on, then we proceed to the next can. They signal with a buzzer or a whistle or they'll yell. The pusher blade pushes the garbage in. A good solid truckload will hold anywhere from eight thousand to twelve thousand pounds. If it's wet, it weighs more. Years ago, you had people burning, a lot of people had garbage burners. You would pick up a lot of ashes. Today most of 'em have converted to gas. In place of ashes, you've got cardboard boxes, you've got wood that people aren't burning any more. It's not like years ago, where people used everything. They're not too economy-wise today. They'll throw anything away. You'll see whole packages of meat just thrown into the garbage can without being opened. I don't know if it's spoiled from the store or not. When I first started here, I had nearly thirty alleys in this ward. Today I'm down to nineteen. And we got better trucks today. Just the way things are packaged today. Plastic. You see a lot of plastic bottles, cardboard boxes.

We try to give 'em twice-a-week service, but we can't complete the ward twice a week. Maybe I can go four alleys over. If I had an alley Monday. I might go in that alley Friday. What happens over the weekend? It just lays there.

After you dump your garbage in the hopper, the sweeper blade goes around to sweep it up, and the push blade pushes it in. This is where you get your sound. Does that sound bother you in the morning? (Laughs.) Sometimes it's irritating to me. If someone comes up to you to talk, and the men are working in the back, and they press the lever, you can't hear them. It's aggravating but you get used to it. We come around seven-twenty. Not too many complaints. Usually you're in the same alley the same day, once a week. The people know that you're coming and it doesn't bother them that much.

Some people will throw, will literally throw garbage out of the window—right in the alley. We have finished an alley in the morning and that same afternoon it will look like it wasn't even done. They might have a cardboard carton in the can and garbage all over the alley. People are just not takin' care of it. You get some people that takes care of their property, they'll come out and sweep around their cans. Other people just don't care or maybe they don't know any better.

Some days it's real nice. Other days, when you get off that truck you're tired, that's it! You say all you do is drive all day, but driving can be pretty tiresome—especially when the kids are out of school. They'll run through a gangway into the alley. This is what you have to watch for. Sitting in that cab, you have a lot of blind spots around the truck. This is what gets you. You watch out that you don't hit any of them.

At times you get aggravated, like your truck breaks down and you get a junk as a replacement. This, believe me, you could take home with you. Otherwise, working here, if there's something on your mind, you don't hold anything in. You discuss anything with these guys. Golf, whatever. One of my laborers just bought a new home and I helped him move some of his small stuff. He's helped me around my house, plumbing and painting.

We've got spotters now. It's new. (Laughs.) They're riding around in unmarked cars. They'll turn you in for stopping for coffee. I can't see that. If you have a coffee break in the alley, it's just using a little psychology. You'll get more out of them. But if you're watched continually, you're gonna lay down. There's definitely more watching today, because there was a lot of layin' down on the job. Truthfully, I'd just as soon put in my eight hours a day as easy as possible. It's hard enough comin' to work. I got a good crew, we get along together, but we have our days.

If you're driving all day, you get tired. By the time you get home, fighting the traffic, you'd just like to relax a little bit. But there's always something around the house. You can get home one night and you'll find your kid threw something in the toilet and you gotta shut your mind and take the toilet apart. (Laughs.) My wife drives, so she does most of the shopping. That was my biggest complaint. So now this job is off my hands. I look forward to my weekends. I get in a little golf.

People ask me what I do, I say, "I drive a garbage truck for the city." They call you G-man, or, "How's business, picking up?" Just the standard . . . Or sanitary engineer. I have nothing to be ashamed of. I put in my eight hours. We make a pretty good salary. I feel I earn my money. I can go any place I want. I conduct myself as a gentleman any place I go. My wife is happy, this is the big thing. She doesn't look down at me. I think that's more important than the white-collar guy looking down at me.

They made a crack to my children at school. My kids would just love to see me do something else. I tell 'em, "Honey, this is a good job. There's nothing to be ashamed of. We're not stealin' the money. You have everything you need."

I don't like to have my salary compared to anybody else's. I don't like to hear that we're makin' more than a schoolteacher. I earn my money just as well as they do. A teacher should get more money, but don't take it away from me.

Insert Flap "A" and Throw Away

S. J. Perelman

ONE stifling summer afternoon last August, in the attic of a tiny stone house in Pennsylvania, I made a most interesting discovery: the shortest, cheapest method of inducing a nervous breakdown ever perfected. In this technique, the subject is placed in a sharply sloping attic heated to 340°F and given a mothproof closet known as the Jiffy-Cloz to assemble. The Jiffy-Cloz, procurable at any department store or neighborhood insane asylum, consists of half a dozen gigantic sheets of red cardboard, two plywood doors, a clothes rack, and a packet of staples. With these is included a set of instructions mimeographed in pale-violet ink, fruity with phrases like "Pass Section F through Slot AA, taking care not to fold tabs behind washers (see Fig. 9)." The cardboard is so processed that as the subject struggles convulsively to force the staple through, it suddenly buckles, plunging the staple deep into his thumb. He thereupon springs up with a dolorous cry and smites his knob (Section K) on the rafters (RR). As a final demonic touch, the Jiffy-Cloz people cunningly omit four of the staples necessary to finish the job, so that after indescribable purgatory, the best the subject can possibly achieve is a sleazy, capricious structure which would reduce any self-respecting moth to helpless laughter. The cumulative frustration, the tropical heat, and the soft, ghostly chuckling of the moths are calculated to unseat the strongest mentality.

In a period of rapid technological change, however, it was inevitable that a method as cumbersome as the Jiffy-Cloz would be superseded. It would be superseded at exactly nine-thirty Christmas morning by a device called the Self-Running 10-Inch Scale-Model Delivery-Truck Kit Powered by Magic Motor, costing twenty-nine cents. About nine on that particular morning, I was spread-eagled on my bed, indulging in my favorite sport of mouth-breathing, when a cork fired from a child's air gun mysteriously lodged in my throat. The pellet proved awkward for a while, but I finally ejected it by flailing the little marksman (and his sister, for good measure) until their welkins rang, and sauntered in to breakfast. Before I could choke down a healing fruit juice, my consort, a tall, regal creature indistinguishable from

Cornelia, the Mother of the Gracchi, except that her foot was entangled in a roller skate, swept in. She extended a large, unmistakable box covered with diagrams.

"Now don't start making excuses," she whined. "It's just a simple cardboard toy. The directions are on the back—"

"Look, dear," I interrupted, rising hurriedly and pulling on my overcoat, "it clean slipped my mind. I'm supposed to take a lesson in crosshatching at Zim's School of Cartooning today."

"On Christmas?" she asked suspiciously.

"Yes, it's the only time they could fit me in," I countered glibly. "This is the big week for crosshatching, you know, between Christmas and New Year's."

"Do you think you ought to go in your pajamas?" she asked.

"Oh, that's O.K.," I smiled. "We often work in our pajamas up at Zim's. Well, goodbye now. If I'm not home by Thursday, you'll find a cold snack in the safe-deposit box." My subterfuge, unluckily, went for naught, and in a trice I was sprawled on the nursery floor, surrounded by two lambkins and ninety-eight segments of the Self-Running 10-Inch Scale-Model Delivery-Truck Construction Kit.

The theory of the kit was simplicity itself, easily intelligible to Kettering of General Motors, Professor Millikan, or any first-rate physicist. Taking as my starting point the only sentence I could comprehend, "Fold down on all lines marked 'fold down'; fold up on all lines marked 'fold up,'" I set the children to work. In a few moments, my skin was suffused with a delightful tingling sensation and I was ready for the second phase, lightly referred to in the directions as "Preparing the Spring Motor Unit." As nearly as I could determine after twenty minutes of mumbling, the Magic Motor ("No Electricity—No Batteries—Nothing to Wind—Motor Never Wears Out") was an accordion-pleated affair operating by torsion, attached to the axles. "It is necessary," said the text, "to cut a slight notch in each of the axles with a knife (see Fig. C.). To find the exact place to cut this notch, lay one of the axles over diagram at bottom of page."

"Well, *now* we're getting some place!" I boomed, with a false gusto that deceived nobody. "Here, Buster, run in and get Daddy a knife."

"I dowanna," quavered the boy, backing away. "You always cut yourself at this stage." I gave the wee fellow an indulgent pat on the head that flattened it slightly, to teach him civility, and commandeered a long, serrated bread knife from the kitchen. "Now watch me closely, children," I ordered. "We place the axle on the diagram as in Fig. C, applying a strong downward pressure on the knife handle at all times." The axle must have been a factory second, because an instant later I was in the bathroom grinding my teeth in agony and attempting to stanch the flow of blood. Ultimately, I succeeded in contriving a rough bandage and slipped back into the nursery without awaking the children's suspicions. An agreeable surprise awaited me. Displaying a mechanical aptitude clearly inherited from their sire, the rascals had put together the chassis of the delivery truck.

"Very good indeed," I complimented (naturally, one has to exaggerate praise to develop a child's self-confidence). "Let's see—what's the next step? Ah, yes, 'Lock into box shape by inserting tabs C, D, E, F, G, H, J, K, and L into slots C, D, E, F, G, H, J, K, and L. Ends of front axle should be pushed through holes A and B.'" While marshalling the indicated parts in their proper order, I emphasized to my rapt listeners the necessity of patience and perseverance. "Haste makes waste, you know," I reminded them. "Rome wasn't built in a day. Remember, your daddy isn't always going to be here to show you."

"Where *are* you going to be?" they demanded.

"In the movies, if I can arrange it," I snarled. Poising tabs C, D, E, F, G, H, J, K, and L in one hand and the corresponding slots in the other, I essayed a union of the two, but in vain. The moment I made one set fast and tackled another, tab and slot would part company, thumbing their noses at me. Although the children were too immature to understand, I saw in a flash where the trouble lay. Some idiotic employee at the factory had punched out the wrong design, probably out of sheer spite. So that was the game, eh? I set my lips in a grim line and, throwing one hundred and fifty-seven pounds of fighting fat into the effort, pounded the component parts into a homogeneous mass.

"There," I said with a gasp, "that's close enough. Now then, who wants candy? One, two, three—everybody off to the candy store!"

"We wanna finish the delivery truck!" they wailed. "Mummy, he won't let us finish the delivery truck!" Threats, cajolery, bribes were of no avail. In their jungle code, a twenty-nine-cent gewgaw bulked larger than a parent's love. Realizing that I was dealing with a pair of monomaniacs, I determined to show them who was master and wildly began locking the cardboard units helter-skelter, without any regard for the directions. When sections refused to fit, I gouged them with my nails and forced them together, cackling shrilly. The side panels collapsed; with a bestial oath, I drove a safety pin through them and lashed them to the roof. I used paper clips, bobby pins, anything I could lay my hands on. My fingers fairly flew and my breath whistled in my throat. "You want a delivery truck, do you?" I panted. "All right, I'll show you!" As merciful blackness closed in, I was on my hands and knees, bunting the infernal thing along with my nose and whinnying, "Roll, confound you, roll!"

"Absolute quiet," a carefully modulated voice was saying, "and fifteen of the white tablets every four hours." I opened my eyes carefully in the darkened room. Dimly I picked out a knife-like character actor in a Vandyke beard and pencil-striped pants folding a stethoscope into his bag. "Yes," he added thoughtfully, "if we play our cards right, this ought to be a long, expensive recovery." From far away, I could hear my wife's voice bravely trying to control her anxiety.

"What if he becomes restless, Doctor?"

"Get him a detective story," returned the leech. "Or better still, a nice, soothing picture puzzle—something he can do with his hands."

It's Plain Hard Work
That Does It

Charles Edison

(Originally entitled "My Most Unforgettable Character: Thomas Edison")

SHUFFLING about his laboratory at Menlo Park, New Jersey, a shock of hair over one side of his forehead, sharp blue eyes sparkling, stains and chemical burns on his wrinkled clothing, Thomas Alva Edison never looked like a man whose inventions had revolutionized the world in less than his lifetime. Certainly he never acted like it. Once when a visiting dignitary asked him whether he had received many medals and awards, he said, "Oh yes, Mom's got a couple of quarts of them up at the house." "Mom" was his wife, my mother.

Yet every day, to those of us who were close to him, he demonstrated what a giant among men he was. Great as were his contributions to mankind—he patented a record 1,093 inventions in his lifetime—it is not for these I remember him, but for his matchless courage, his imagination and determination, his humility and wit. At times, he was just plain mischievous.

Because of his prodigious work schedule, his home life was relatively restricted. But he did find time to go fishing, motoring, and the like with the family, and when we children were young to play parchisi and romp on the floor with us. One thing I remember well is Independence Day at Glenmont, our three-story gabled home in West Orange, New Jersey, which is now a national monument. This was Father's favorite holiday. He might start by throwing a firecracker into a barrel at dawn, awakening us and the neighbors as well. Then we would shoot off fireworks in varying combinations all day.

"Mom's not going to like it," he would say mischievously, "but let's put twenty together and see what happens."

Always Father encouraged our experimentation and exploration. He provided clocks and other gadgets to tinker with, and kidded, challenged and questioned us into doing things. He had me washing beakers in his chemical laboratory when I was six, and when I was ten he helped me get started building a full-sized car. It never had a body, but it did have a little two-cycle marine engine and a belt drive. It worked. We kids had a lot of fun with it. Several times my brother Theodore and I played "polo" on the lawn with croquet mallets and autos—and nobody but Mother and the gardener objected.

At home or at work, Father seemed to have a knack for motivating others. He could and often did give orders but he preferred to inspire people by his own example. This was one of the secrets of his success. For he was not, as many believe, a scientist who worked in solitude in a laboratory. Once he had marketed his first successful invention—a stock ticker and printer—for $40,000, he began employing chemists, mathematicians, machinists, anyone whose talents he thought might help him solve a knotty problem. Thus he married science to industry with the "team" research concept, which is standard today.

Sometimes, during his recurrent financial crises, Father couldn't pay his men. But, as one recalled: "It didn't matter. We all came to work just the same. We wouldn't stay away."

Father himself usually worked eighteen or more hours a day. "Accomplishing something provides the only real satisfaction in life," he told us. His widely reported ability to get by with no more than four hours' sleep—plus an occasional catnap—was no exaggeration. "Sleep," he maintained, "is like a drug. Take too much at a time and it makes you dopey. You lose time, vitality, and opportunities."

His successes are well known. In the phonograph, which he invented when he was thirty, he captured sound on records; his incandescent bulb lighted the world. He invented the microphone, mimeograph, medical fluoroscope, the nickel-iron-alkaline storage battery, and the movies. He made the inventions of others—the telephone, telegraph, typewriter—commercially practical. He conceived our entire electrical distribution system.

It is sometimes asked, "Didn't he ever fail?" The answer is yes. Thomas Edison knew failure frequently. His first patent, when he was all but penniless, was for an electric vote-recorder, but maneuver-minded legislators refused to buy it. Once he had his entire fortune tied up in machinery for a magnetic separation process for low-grade iron ore—only to have it made obsolete and uneconomical by the opening of the rich Mesabi Range. But he never hesitated out of fear of failure.

"Shucks," he told a discouraged co-worker during one trying

series of experiments, "we haven't failed. We now know a thousand things that won't work, so we're that much closer to finding what will."

His attitude toward money (or lack of it) was similar. He considered it as a raw material, like metal, to be used rather than amassed, and so he kept plowing his funds into new projects. Several times he was all but bankrupt. But he refused to let dollar signs govern his actions.

One day at his ore-crushing mill, Father became dissatisfied with the way a rock-crusher machine was working. "Give her another turn of speed," he ordered the operator.

"I dassn't," came the reply. "She'll break."

Father turned to the foreman. "How much did she cost, Ed?"

"Twenty-five thousand dollars."

"Have we got that much money in the bank? All right, go ahead and give her another notch."

The operator increased the power. And then once more. "She's pounding somethin' awful," he warned. "She'll break our heads!"

"Damn our heads," Father shouted. "Let her out!"

As the pounding became louder, they began to retreat. Suddenly there was a crash and pieces flew in all directions. The crusher was broken.

"Well," the foreman asked Father, "what did you learn from that?"

"Why," said Father with a smile, "that I can put on 40 percent more power than the builder said she could stand—all but that last notch. Now I can build one just as good, and get more production out of it."

I especially recall a freezing December night in 1914, at a time when still-unfruitful experiments on the nickel-iron-alkaline storage battery, to which Father had devoted much of ten years, had put him on a financial tightrope. Only profits from movie and record production were supporting the laboratory. On that December evening the cry of "Fire!" echoed through the plant. Spontaneous combustion had occurred in the film room. Within moments all the packing compounds, celluloid for records, film, and other flammable goods had gone up with a whoosh. Fire companies from eight towns arrived, but the heat was so intense, and the water pressure so low, that the fire hoses had no effect.

When I couldn't find Father, I became concerned. Was he safe? With all his assets going up in smoke, would his will be broken? He was sixty-seven, no age to begin anew. Then I saw him in the plant yard, running toward me.

"Where's Mom?" he shouted. "Go get her! Tell her to get her friends! They'll never see a fire like this again!"

At 5:30 the next morning, with the fire barely under control, he called his employees together and announced, "We're rebuilding." One man was told to lease all the machine shops in the area. Another, to obtain a wrecking crane from the Erie Railroad. Then, almost as an afterthought he added, "Oh, by the way. Anybody know where we can get some money?"

"You can always make capital out of disaster," he said. "We've just cleared out a bunch of old rubbish. We'll build bigger and better on the ruins." With that he rolled up his coat, curled up on a table, and immediately fell asleep.

His remarkable succession of inventions made him appear to possess almost magical powers, so that he was called "The Wizard of Menlo Park." The notion alternately amused and angered him.

"Wizard?" he would say. "Pshaw. It's plain hard work that does it." Or, his much quoted statement: "Genius is one percent inspiration and 99 percent perspiration." Laziness, mental laziness in particular, tried his patience. He kept a statement attributed to Sir Joshua Reynolds hanging prominently in his laboratory and factories: "There is no expedient to which a man will not resort to avoid the real labor of thinking."

Father never changed his sense of values or his hat size. In Boston, when the power failed at the opening of the first American theater to use incandescent lights, he doffed his tie and tails (which he detested) and unhesitatingly headed for the basement to help find the trouble. In Paris, shortly after receiving the Legion of Honor, he quietly removed the tiny red rosette from his lapel, lest friends "think I'm a dude."

After the death of his first wife, Father married the woman who became my mother, Mina Miller. In her he found a perfect complement. She was poised, gracious, self-sufficient; she willingly adjusted to Father's busy schedule. Theirs was a marriage that warmed all whom it touched. Father's diary, the only one he kept (covering nine days in 1885, before they were married), indicated how smitten he was by her. "Got to thinking of Mina and came near being run over by a streetcar," he confessed.

When he proposed, it was in Morse code, which she had learned during their courtship. In later life, when he worked at a desk at home, she was at hers beside him, usually busy with civic projects, in which she was extremely active.

Thomas Edison has sometimes been represented as uneducated. Actually he had only six months of formal schooling, but under his mother's tutelage in Port Huron, Michigan, he had read such classics as *Decline and Fall of the Roman Empire* at the age of eight or nine. After becoming a vendor and newsboy on the Grand Trunk Railroad, he spent whole days in the Detroit Free Library—which he read "from top to bottom." In our home he always had books and magazines, as well as half a dozen daily newspapers.

From childhood, this man who was to accomplish so much was almost totally deaf. He could hear only the loudest noises and shouts, but this did not bother him. "I haven't heard a bird sing since I was twelve," he once said. "But rather than a handicap my deafness probably has been beneficial." He believed it drove him early to reading, enabled him to concentrate, and shut him off from small talk.

People asked him why he didn't invent a hearing aid. Father always replied, "How much have you heard in the last twenty-four hours that you couldn't do without?" He followed this up with: "A man who has to shout can never tell a lie."

He enjoyed music, and if the arrangement emphasized the melody, he could "listen" by biting a pencil and placing the other end of it against a phonograph cabinet. The vibrations and rhythm came through perfectly. The phonograph, incidentally, was his favorite of all his inventions.

Although his deafness required shouted conversation or written questions and answers, reporters enjoyed interviewing him for his pithy, penetrating comments. Once, asked what advice he had for youth, he replied, "Youth doesn't take advice." He never accepted happiness or contentment as worthwhile goals. "Show me a thoroughly satisfied man," he said, "and I will show you a failure." Asked if technological progress could lend to overproduction, he replied, "There cannot be overproduction of anything which men and women want. And their wants are unlimited, except by the size of their stomachs!"

Many tributes were paid Father but two pleased him especially. One came on October 21, 1929, the golden anniversary of the incandescent lamp, when Henry Ford re-created Father's Menlo Park, New Jersey, laboratory in Dearborn, Michigan, to be a permanent shrine in Ford's vast exhibit of Americana at Greenfield Village. This was Ford's expression of gratitude to Father for his words of encouragement when doubt and despair almost turned Ford from the development of his first auto. We could see by his smile that Father was deeply touched.

The other outstanding salute came in 1928, in his own library-laboratory-office in West Orange. He had received honors and medals from many nations. But it was particularly gratifying when, on this occasion, Father was awarded a special gold "Medal of the Congress of the United States" in recognition of his achievements.

He never retired. Nor did he have qualms about the onset of old age. At the age of eighty, he entered a science completely new to him, botany. His goal: to find a native source of rubber. After testing and classifying seventeen thousand varieties of plants, he and his assistants succeeded in devising a method of extracting latex from goldenrod in substantial quantities.

At eighty-three, hearing that Newark Airport was the busiest in the East, he dragged Mother down there to "see how a real airport works." When he saw his first helicopter, he beamed, "That's the way I always thought it should be done." And he started sketching improvements for the little-known whirlybird.

Finally, at eighty-four, ill with uremic poisoning, he started to fail. Scores of reporters arrived to keep vigil. Hourly the news was relayed to them: "The light still burns." But at 3:24 A.M. on October 18, 1931, word came: "The light is out."

The final salute, on the day of his funeral, was to be the cut-off of all electric current in the nation for one minute. But this was deemed too costly and dangerous. Instead, only certain lights were dimmed. The wheels of progress were not stilled, even for an instant.

Thomas Edison, I am sure, would have wanted it that way.

Steelworker

Trudy Pax Farr

MY first day. The BOP (Basic Oxygen Process) Shop towers some six or seven stories. Everywhere there is equipment of gigantic proportions. Ladles, cranes, transfer cars. We workers are dwarfed beside them. Forklift trucks and bulldozers run around like beetles.

I stand mesmerized when the huge furnace tips and slowly pours out its liquid fire—what other name can I give that brilliant soup? "Don't look at it," another worker says, "you need these," and he gives me some small blue-lensed glasses that I can clip on my safety glasses and flip up or down as I need. As the steel flows from the tap hole of the furnace into the waiting ladle, a sunset glow sweeps over everything and, for a brief moment, there is color in this drab, relentlessly gray building.

Many feet above—I can barely make out the operator in the cab—runs the crane, its runway spanning the width of the building. It comes now, and with much creaking and straining, laboriously lifts the filled ladle. When it does, some steel sloshes over and a glowing puddle sits on the ground after the crane glides away.

I become a burner. I don a stiff metalliclike coat and leggings, strap leather gaiters over shoes. A welder-type shield over my face, leather one-fingered mitts for my hands. All to protect me from the "sparks" (in fact, small droplets of hot steel) that shower down when oxygen, flame, and air meet molten steel. Still, those sparks find their way down my shirt front, into my gloves. At first, I stop to inspect each small burn, but before long I do as the seasoned burners do: simply shake the spark out of my glove the best I can, hold my shirt away from my body and let it tumble down, and continue at the job. Under all that fireproof clothing, my T-shirt and bra are filled with small burn holes. My hands are pock-marked.

Steel: durable, impregnable, indestructible. I cut through it like butter. At a touch, the flame of my torch turns that sturdy mass of steel into flowing liquid. What power!

Sometimes I cut scrap—old rods from the stoppers that close the opening on the ladles. Sometimes I help prepare molds for the next batch of steel—I cut off the steel that has spilled over the edges and has hardened there. Sometimes I'm called to the ladle liners—steel has worked its way in between the bricks of the ladle lining and now they need to get those "frozen bricks" out. (This is tricky: Cut the spilled steel, but not the ladle that it's attached to.) Sometimes I work the mixers (large heated drums that hold the molten iron until the furnaces are ready for it)—then it's iron, not steel, that we cut away. It has sloshed around the opening, building up layer after layer until we need to clean away big chunks. Sometimes there are spills on the railroad tracks—a mold full of molten steel has toppled and the hardened metal has to be cleared. All these jobs are small and are done with a hand-held torch.

But more often than not, I work in the "strawberry patch." What a colorful name for yet another ugly spot: an area just outside the BOP Shop where they dump the leftovers from ladles—big bowl-shaped chunks of steel and sediment that must be cut in half before a crane can lift them. Then I work with an unwieldy fifteen-foot rod that can reach far into the crevice I create as I burn. Out of that crevice comes a waterfall of fantastic colors. Through my blue-tinted glasses (now I use those glasses my fellow worker gave me on that first day), I watch it flow like candle wax: red, bright orange, magenta—snaking out, layer upon layer, each quickly fading to a paler shade. A thing of beauty. The only beauty in this gray and dusty place.

One day I meet a photographer—he's come to make an ad for Ford. It will show a spanking-new car springing effortlessly and ready-made from the molten steel. He is surprised to find women working in the mill and asks about burning. I proudly explain the process. Then, "Tell me," he says, "how do you breathe in here?" How indeed? I develop a chronic cough.

Little by little, I begin to feel like a real part of the mill crew. I know I have made it when I begin breaking in new workers. Occasionally the new worker is a woman. On those days, the mill seems different: less austere, more hospitable. We relax, work smoothly; we have to answer to no one, have nothing to prove.

I try to befriend some of the old-time women—those left from the days of World War II when women did so many of the mill jobs: welders, track gang, crane operators, observers. I am fascinated with their life stories: how they came to the mill during the war; how they managed to stay on after everyone told them that their patriotic duty of taking a job in the mill was over, that their patriotic duty *now* was to go home and be a full-time wife. But, for the most part, they seem to resent us newcomers. They complain because we have it easier than they did, because we don't work hard enough, because we demand too much. And sometimes because too many of us are black.

We—all of us in the mill—work around the clock. There are no weekends, no holidays. Steelmaking, they tell us, can take no rest. We come and go—at eight, at four, at midnight. We meet briefly, passing the baton, so to speak, of our particular job. If no relief shows up, we stay for an extra turn (shift).

For single mothers with small children, the schedule is pure hell. Some might call it irony; I call it injustice: Single mothers who so desperately need these relatively well-paying jobs have to face impossible conditions. And no exceptions can be made. (Although I've seen a man get a "special schedule" to accommodate his working wife.)

Each week, people cluster around the bulletin board to decipher their schedule for the coming week. Some read it and are silent: pleased or perhaps resigned. Others object. "Sunday, first turn! No way! Let me talk to that scheduler!" And off they stomp to Nurven's office—a small shanty next to the general foreman's. More often than not they soon come back, sit glumly and silently in the shanty. Nurven is not easily persuaded.

Accidents happen everywhere in the mill. But none so gruesome as those in the BOP Shop. I am on the midnight turn when the first fatality happens. I am working in another area, but hear the voice on the intercom. I don't suspect death—the voice is urgent, but not panicky: "Get a foreman down here. We have a problem." In the morning, I learn it was amiable, deliberate, soft-spoken Slow Joe, his forklift truck tipped over by a railroad transfer car. Not long after, there is the remote-control train operator, squashed by the very cars he is manipulating. Then the millwright caught in the huge cables of the crane he was working on. Another millwright crushed when the equipment he is repairing collapses on him. A man burned to death by steel that spills over the edge of the ladle. Each death wrenches me, twists my heart for days. But despite it all, I feel immune. Confident no such thing will happen to me.

Confident, until it happens to a burner.

They tell me about it when I come into the mill for my afternoon turn. A freak accident, they say. He was working on a strawberry, cutting it in half as usual, when the molten steel that had gathered in the crevice "backfired" and spewed out on him. He has third degree burns on most of his body. He is still alive, they say, but barely. Better to die, they say.

I go to the spot where it happened. I stand looking at the half-finished strawberry—a strawberry like any of the dozens I had worked on. I nudge a piece of something on the ground with my metal-tipped shoe. It is a portion of the burner's safety glasses, melted and contorted. And I think: The only reason I'm standing here and not lying in a burn unit somewhere in the city is a question of schedule. I decide I no longer want to be a burner.

I put aside the tools of the burner: torch and striker, rods and hoses. I put aside my fireproof clothing. I take up a trowel and hammer; I become a ladle liner.

The ladle liners' job: Build a floor and wall of firebrick inside the ladle, to keep the molten steel from burning right through the ladle. I heft the eighty-pound bags of cement, mixing it in big drums to make the "soup" that will seal the bricks together. I climb down into the huge container, big enough to hold two hundred tons of molten steel. I slap the bricks in place—clack, clack, clack—one layer, two layers. A wall to hold in all that heat and fire. Like a mason, I tap the brick with my hammer to make it break just so, the exact place, the exact size I need to fit this space, to snug this row.

Some of the ladles come to us direct from the teeming aisle, still hot from the recently poured steel. A pleasant thing on a cold night; not so in the summer.

Steelmaking—that's the heart of it. But the process, despite all our technological know-how, is still a surprisingly seat-of-the-pants operation. The final product is always iffy, and the furnace men are always nervous, often frantic. We try to have as little as possible to do with them, but all our work revolves around them. The ladles we line will carry the steel they create, poured fresh and boiling hot from the furnaces.

A good day—things are perking along. One after another, the torpedo-shaped railroad cars come rolling in, bringing iron from the blast furnace. Iron, scrap, a few bags of this and that dumped into the furnaces. Then what wild rushing sounds: flame and fire, roar and grumble. Steel is being made. Frenzy everywhere. Prepare the molds. Are there enough? On what track shall they be put? Send for the crane: Take this ladle here, bring one from there. Workers pull on their metallic-like coats, ready to approach the heat and fire. On the platform, the steel pourers crook their arms over their faces, a futile attempt to shield themselves from the heat, the glare. They move in quickly, manipulate the flow, take a sample, and move away. Mold after mold is filled with the molten steel.

But not always—things do not always perk. . . .

Then there is time to sit. We gather in the shanty. (A name that reveals historical origins. Now it is no more than a room to the side of the foreman's office.) We talk about many things. (How Americans never live to be a hundred. "Speak for yourself!" says Love, indignant.) About the general foreman. (How he gives you days off, at the drop of a hat. "He don't know no number smaller than three," says Medicine Man.) Stories of the mill, perhaps already told too often, but part of our culture. There's always one newcomer who has not yet heard them. (How Beefco's dentures fell down through the opening in the ladle he was working on, landed in a bucket of mud and slush in front of Casper, who went running to the office, pale as the ghost for whom he is named. How Beefco went to retrieve them, wiped them on his pants, put them back in his mouth . . . How they tied Potato's shoes together while he slept . . . How Richie the foreman got fired for stealing . . . How. . . .)

On those slow days, there's time for a leisurely lunch. We put packets of tacos, jars of soup, and foilwrapped ears of corn on the salamanders, and stand around those drums of burning coke while the food heats. Once there was even a whole fish, wrapped and cooked, then spread open for everyone to feast on.

In summer, the heat is unbearable: In addition to nature's heat, we have the steelmaking heat and our heavy protective clothing. Everyone has their theory on how to combat it. Ice cubes in drinks, under hard hats, down shirts. The ice machine they installed in the shanty works overtime. But College Joe makes pot after pot of strong coffee on his little hot plate. "The hotter it gets," he insists, "the more coffee you hafta drink."

Seasons come and go in the mill. As far as I know, they will go on forever.

But one day, when the new schedule appears on the board, my name is on a separate list—the one entitled "furlough." I don't mind. This has happened before, and it is a welcome break. A chance to forget about shift work, a chance to live a normal life for a week or two. There are rumors that this layoff is bigger, farther-reaching, but I dismiss those rumors. I have just invested in a pair of new metatarsal shoes—I am sure I will be using them for a long time. I walk to the locker room in my new shoes, put them and the rest of my work clothes in my locker, walk out the gate, and never set foot there again. The big layoff has hit.

Reporters begin trekking to this far southeast corner of Chicago—an area foreign to most of them. Nothing of consequence happens here. But now! Thousands laid off in one fell swoop. Mills closing with hardly a day's notice.

But what have they come to investigate? They nod listlessly, pencils suspended over their notebooks when we talk of women's hopes dashed, or returning to humdrum low-paying jobs. A Santa-less Christmas—that is what they want to hear. A starving child, foreclosures, suicides—these are stories they drool over. And there *are* those stories. When one surfaces, they perk up, smile. They begin scribbling in their notebooks.

Despite all the attention, we feel invisible to the nonsteelworker world. For some time, among ourselves, we keep our identity: We continue to meet at the union hall; government cheese, milk, and honey are distributed; a job training program is started. But there is not much hope. Other mills—and other industries, too—are closing. Even workers with training—machinists, plumbers, welders, electricians—find it hard to get a job. Workers are being shepherded through a funnel into the shrinking job pool. A few make it through. Most are left to flounder. There is a feeling of life having come to a halt; a feeling of depression: What will become of us, our community? A feeling of betrayal: So many loyal years given to the mill; now the company turns its back.

Little by little, our ties weaken, and we scatter.

What has happened to that small group of women who once called themselves steelworkers? I have lost track of all but a handful.

Some sought jobs similar to the mill—construction, apprenticeships. A few succeeded; most didn't. Some went back to previous jobs. Jobs that, when you came right down to it, they preferred all along. Jobs that pay less, but are less dirty, less dangerous, and, most importantly, have a decent work schedule—a schedule more compatible with raising kids. Some (like me) went back to school, seeking security and stability in nursing, computing, word processing, teaching. A few fled the Rust Belt, along with the industries, looking for the much-touted jobs in the Sunbelt. I don't know what happened to them.

Sometimes, when I go past that deserted parking lot, now overgrown with weeds, the fences battered and falling, and I see the BOP Shop looming there just beyond, I recall the days at the mill. Then a part of me sighs with relief—the part of me that hated the midnight turns, the dirt, the danger, the harassment, the chaotic life. But another part of me is rather nostalgic—the part that felt the satisfaction of overcoming trepidation, that liked being a part of something BIG. The part of me that enjoyed so much the banter, the camaraderie, the oneness of the mill life. And if today, I were offered a chance to do it all over again, I'm not at all sure what my answer would be.

Teamwork

Michael Jordan

IT seems our society tends to glamorize individual levels of success without taking the entire process into consideration. Football is a prime example.

I think football is a backward sport.

Here you have a guy, the quarterback, who is very intelligent and is probably capable of carrying the team. But he can't do that if he doesn't have the protection of the guards and tackles in front of him. Yet those guys make pennies while the quarterback makes nickels. That doesn't make any sense. If you don't have those guys up front, that nickel isn't worth a penny.

It works the same way in a corporation. What if you have a CEO with a great idea, but he doesn't have the people to make it happen? If you don't have all the pieces in place, particularly at the front lines, that idea doesn't mean a thing. You can have the greatest salespeople in the world, but if the people making the product aren't any good, no one will buy it.

On the Bulls, we had two guys with distinct abilities in Bill Cartwright and John Paxson. And we found a way to use those talents within the framework of our team. It's the same with workers on the lower end of the corporate ladder. Managers, just like basketball coaches, have to find a way to utilize those individual talents in the best interests of the company.

When we started winning championships, there was an understanding among all twelve players about what our roles were. We knew our responsibilities and we knew our capabilities.

We knew, for example, that we wanted to go to Bill early and try to get him into the flow of the game. We knew that if John hit his first shot it would open things up for Scottie Pippen, B.J. Armstrong, and myself. Those were the kinds of things we had to understand and accept if we were going to win championships.

It took us a period of time to understand that. It's a selfless process, and in our society sometimes it's hard to come to grips with filling a role instead of trying to be a superstar. There is a tendency to ignore or fail to respect all the parts that make the whole thing possible.

Naturally there are going to be some ups and downs, particularly if you have individuals trying to achieve at a high level. But when we stepped in between the lines, we knew what we were capable of doing. When a pressure situation presented itself, we were plugged into one another as a cohesive unit. That's why we were able to come back so often and win so many close games.

And that's why we were able to beat more talented teams. There are plenty of teams in every sport that have great players and never win titles. Most of the time, those players aren't willing to sacrifice for the greater good of the team. The funny thing is, in the end, their unwillingness to sacrifice only makes individual goals more difficult to achieve.

The one thing I was taught at North Carolina, and one thing that I believe to the fullest, is that if you think and achieve as a team, the individual accolades will take care of themselves.

Me? I'd rather have five guys with less talent who are willing to come together as a team than five guys who consider themselves stars and aren't willing to sacrifice.

Talent wins games, but teamwork and intelligence win championships.

Hephaistos Forges Achilles' Shield

Homer

HEPHAISTOS is the Greek god of fire- and metalworking. In Homer's epic the Iliad, Thetis, Achilles' *mother, asks Hephaistos to make armor and a shield to protect her son.*

'Why is it, Thetis of the light robes, you have come to our house
    now?
We honour you and love you; but you have not come much
    before this.
Speak forth what is in your mind. My heart is urgent to do it
if I can, and if it is a thing that can be accomplished.'
    Then in turn Thetis answered him, letting the tears fall:
'Hephaistos, is there among all the goddesses on Olympos
one who in her heart has endured so many grim sorrows
as the griefs Zeus, son of Kronos, has given me beyond others?
Of all the other sisters of the sea he gave me to a mortal,
to Peleus, Aiakos' son, and I had to endure mortal marriage
though much against my will. And now he, broken by mournful
old age, lies away in his halls. Yet I have other troubles.
For since he has given me a son to bear and to raise up
conspicuous among heroes, and he shot up like a young tree,
I nurtured him, like a tree grown in the pride of the orchard.
I sent him away in the curved ships to the land of Ilion
to fight with the Trojans; but I shall never again receive him
won home again to his country and into the house of Peleus.
Yet while I see him live and he looks on the sunlight, he has
sorrows, and though I go to him I can do nothing to help him.
And the girl the sons of the Achaians chose out for his honour
powerful Agamemnon took her away again out of his hands.
For her his heart has been wasting in sorrow; but meanwhile
    the Trojans
pinned the Achaians against their grounded ships, and would
    not
let them win outside, and the elders of the Argives entreated
my son, and named the many glorious gifts they would give him.

But at that time he refused himself to fight the death from
    them;
nevertheless he put his own armour upon Patroklos
and sent him into the fighting, and gave many men to go with him.
All day they fought about the Skaian Gates, and on that day
they would have stormed the city, if only Phoibos Apollo
had not killed the fighting son of Menoitios there in the first ranks
after he had wrought much damage, and given the glory to Hektor.
Therefore now I come to your knees; so might you be willing
to give me for my short-lived son a shield and a helmet
and two beautiful greaves fitted with clasps for the ankles
and a corselet. What he had was lost with his steadfast companion
when the Trojans killed him. Now my son lies on the ground,
    heart sorrowing.'
  Hearing her the renowned smith of the strong arms answered
    her:
'Do not fear. Let not these things be a thought in your mind.
And I wish that I could hide him away from death and its sorrow
at that time when his hard fate comes upon him, as surely
as there shall be fine armour for him, such as another
man out of many men shall wonder at, when he looks on it.'
  So he spoke, and left her there, and went to his bellows.
He turned these toward the fire and gave them their orders for
    working.
And the bellows, all twenty of them, blew on the crucibles,
from all directions blasting forth wind to blow the flames high
now as he hurried to be at this place and now at another,
wherever Hephaistos might wish them to blow, and the work
    went forward.
He cast on the fire bronze which is weariless, and tin with it
and valuable gold, and silver, and thereafter set forth
upon its standard the great anvil, and gripped in one hand
the ponderous hammer, while in the other he grasped the pincers.
  First of all he forged a shield that was huge and heavy,
elaborating it about, and threw around it a shining
triple rim that glittered, and the shield strap was cast of silver.
There were five folds composing the shield itself, and upon it
he elaborated many things in his skill and craftsmanship.
  He made the earth upon it, and the sky, and the sea's water,
and the tireless sun, and the moon waxing into her fullness,
and on it all the constellations that festoon the heavens,
the Pleiades and the Hyades and the strength of Orion

and the Bear, whom men give also the name of the Wagon,
who turns about in a fixed place and looks at Orion
and she alone is never plunged in the wash of the Ocean.
    On it he wrought in all their beauty two cities of mortal
men. And there were marriages in one, and festivals.
They were leading the brides along the city from their maiden
    chambers
under the flaring of torches, and the loud bride song was arising.
The young men followed the circles of the dance, and among them
the flutes and lyres kept up their clamour as in the meantime
the women standing each at the door of her court admired them.
The people were assembled in the market place, where a quarrel
had arisen, and two men were disputing over the blood price
for a man who had been killed. One man promised full restitution
in a public statement, but the other refused and would accept
    nothing.
Both then made for an arbitrator, to have a decision;
and people were speaking up on either side, to help both men.
But the heralds kept the people in hand, as meanwhile the elders
were in session on benches of polished stone in the sacred circle
and held in their hands the staves of the heralds who lift their
    voices.
The two men rushed before these, and took turns speaking
    their cases,
and between them lay on the ground two talents of gold, to be
    given
to that judge who in this case spoke the straightest opinion.
    But around the other city were lying two forces of armed men
shining in their war gear. For one side counsel was divided
whether to storm and sack, or share between both sides the
    property
and all the possessions the lovely citadel held hard within it.
But the city's people were not giving way, and armed for an
    ambush.
Their beloved wives and their little children stood on the rampart
to hold it, and with them the men with age upon them, but
    meanwhile
the others went out. And Ares led them, and Pallas Athene.
These were gold, both, and golden raiment upon them, and they
    were
beautiful and huge in their armour, being divinities,
and conspicuous from afar, but the people around them were
    smaller.

These, when they were come to the place that was set for their
    ambush,
in a river, where there was a watering place for all animals,
there they sat down in place shrouding themselves in the bright
    bronze.
But apart from these were sitting two men to watch for the rest
    of them
and waiting until they could see the sheep and the shambling
    cattle,
who appeared presently, and two herdsmen went along with them
playing happily on pipes, and took no thought of the treachery.
Those others saw them, and made a rush, and quickly thereafter
cut off on both sides the herds of cattle and the beautiful
flocks of shining sheep, and killed the shepherds upon them.
But the other army, as soon as they heard the uproar arising
from the cattle, as they sat in their councils, suddenly mounted
behind their light-foot horses, and went after, and soon
    overtook them.
These stood their ground and fought a battle by the banks of
    the river,
and they were making casts at each other with their spears
    bronze-headed;
and Hate was there with Confusion among them, and Death the
    destructive;
she was holding a live man with a new wound, and another
one unhurt, and dragged a dead man by the feet through the
    carnage.
The clothing upon her shoulders showed strong red with the
    men's blood.
All closed together like living men and fought with each other
and dragged away from each other the corpses of those who had
    fallen.
   He made upon it a soft field, the pride of the tilled land,
wide and triple-ploughed, with many ploughmen upon it
who wheeled their teams at the turn and drove them in either
    direction.
And as these making their turn would reach the end-strip of the
    field,
a man would come up to them at this point and hand them a
    flagon
of honey-sweet wine, and they would turn again to the furrows
in their haste to come again to the end-strip of the deep field.

The earth darkened behind them and looked like earth that has
    been ploughed.
though it was gold. Such was the wonder of the shield's forging.
    He made on it the precinct of a king, where the labourers
were reaping, with the sharp reaping hooks in their hands. Of
    the cut swathes
some fell along the lines of reaping, one after another,
while the sheaf-binders caught up others and tied them with
    bind-ropes.
There were three sheaf-binders who stood by, and behind them
were children picking up the cut swathes, and filled their arms
    with them
and carried and gave them always; and by them the king in silence
and holding his staff stood near the line of the reapers, happily.
And apart and under a tree the heralds made a feast ready
and trimmed a great ox they had slaughtered. Meanwhile the
    women
scattered, for the workmen to eat, abundant white barley.
    He made on it a great vineyard heavy with clusters,
lovely and in gold, but the grapes upon it were darkened
and the vines themselves stood out through poles of silver.
    About them
he made a field-ditch of dark metal, and drove all around this
a fence of tin; and there was only one path to the vineyard,
and along it ran the grape-bearers for the vineyard's stripping.
Young girls and young men, in all their light-hearted innocence,
carried the kind, sweet fruit away in their woven baskets,
and in their midst a youth with a singing lyre played charmingly
upon it for them, and sang the beautiful song for Linos
in a light voice, and they followed him, and with singing and
    whistling
and light dance-steps of their feet kept time to the music.
    He made upon it a herd of horn-straight oxen. The cattle
were wrought of gold and of tin, and thronged in speed and with
    lowing
out of the dung of the farmyard to a pasturing place by a
    sounding
river, and beside the moving field of a reed bed.
The herdsmen were of gold who went along with the cattle,
four of them, and nine dogs shifting their feet followed them.
But among the foremost of the cattle two formidable lions
had caught hold of a bellowing bull, and he with loud lowings

was dragged away, as the dogs and the young men went in
　　pursuit of him.
But the two lions, breaking open the hide of the great ox,
gulped the black blood and the inward guts, as meanwhile the
　　herdsmen
were in the act of setting and urging the quick dogs on them.
But they, before they could get their teeth in, turned back from
　　the lions,
but would come and take their stand very close, and bayed, and
　　kept clear.
　　And the renowned smith of the strong arms made on it a
　　meadow
large and in a lovely valley for the glimmering sheepflocks,
with dwelling places upon it, and covered shelters, and sheepfolds.
　　And the renowned smith of the strong arms made elaborate
　　on it
a dancing floor, like that which once in the wide spaces of Knosos
Daidalos built for Ariadne of the lovely tresses.
And there were young men on it and young girls, sought for
　　their beauty
with gifts of oxen, dancing, and holding hands at the wrist. These
wore, the maidens long light robes, but the men wore tunics
of finespun work and shining softly, touched with olive oil.
And the girls wore fair garlands on their heads, while the young
　　men
carried golden knives that hung from sword-belts of silver.
At whiles on their understanding feet they would run very
　　lightly,
as when a potter crouching makes trial of his wheel, holding
it close in his hands, to see if it will run smooth. At another
time they would form rows, and run, rows crossing each other.
And around the lovely chorus of dancers stood a great multitude
happily watching, while among the dancers two acrobats
led the measures of song and dance revolving among them.
　　He made on it the great strength of the Ocean River
which ran around the uttermost rim of the shield's strong
　　structure.
　　Then after he had wrought this shield, which was huge and
　　heavy,
he wrought for him a corselet brighter than fire in its shining,
and wrought him a helmet, massive and fitting close to his
　　temples,

lovely and intricate work, and laid a gold top-ridge along it,
and out of pliable tin wrought him leg-armour. Thereafter
when the renowned smith of the strong arms had finished the
    armour
he lifted it and laid it before the mother of Achilleus.
And she like a hawk came sweeping down from the snows of
    Olympos
and carried with her the shining armour, the gift of Hephaistos.

Working-Class Hero

Alan Jackson and Don Sampson

A calloused right hand
Holds a shiny gold watch
For thirty years spent on the clock
But you won't see no tears
From this working-class hero
He's always been hard as a rock

But he knows he's too old
To really start over
Besides he just wouldn't know how
I guess he's just glad
That he's not alone
But he's got to wonder what now

Cause there's no wall of fame for that working-class hero
No statue carved out of stone
And his greatest reward is the love of a woman
And his children
So after he's gone
That old working-class hero lives on

Well, that three-bedroom house
He built in the 50's
Seems so much bigger today
With just him and mama
And not many bills
Cause the kids moved away

What he's done with his life
Might not be remembered
But he's got every right to be proud
Cause the blood sweatin' years
Of this working-class hero
Is really what livin's about

Cause there's no wall of fame for that working-class hero
No statue carved out of stone
And his greatest reward is the love of a woman
And his children
So after he's gone
That old working-class hero lives on
Yea, that working-class hero lives on

The Toolmaker Unemployed

Martín Espada

—Connecticut River Valley, 1992

The toolmaker
is sixty years old,
unemployed
since the letter
from his boss
at the machine shop.

He carries
a cooler of soda
everywhere,
so as not to carry
a flask of whiskey.

During the hours
of his shift,
he is building a barn
with borrowed lumber
or hacking at trees
in the yard.

The family watches
and listens to talk
of a bullet
in the forehead,
maybe for himself,
maybe for the man
holding the second mortgage.

Sometimes
he stares down
into his wallet.

The Death of the Hired Man

Robert Frost

Mary sat musing on the lamp-flame at the table,
Waiting for Warren. When she heard his step,
She ran on tiptoe down the darkened passage
To meet him in the doorway with the news
And put him on his guard, "Silas is back."
She pushed him outward with her through the door
And shut it after her. "Be kind," she said.
She took the market things from Warren's arms
And set them on the porch, then drew him down
To sit beside her on the wooden steps.

"When was I ever anything but kind to him?
But I'll not have the fellow back," he said.
"I told him so last haying, didn't I?
If he left then, I said, that ended it.
What good is he? Who else will harbor him
At his age for the little he can do?
What help he is there's no depending on.
Off he goes always when I need him most.
He thinks he ought to earn a little pay,
Enough at least to buy tobacco with,
So he won't have to beg and be beholden.
'All right,' I say, 'I can't afford to pay
Any fixed wages, though I wish I could.'
'Someone else can.' 'Then someone else will have to.'
I shouldn't mind his bettering himself
If that was what it was. You can be certain,
When he begins like that, there's someone at him
Trying to coax him off with pocket money—
In haying time, when any help is scarce.
In winter he comes back to us. I'm done."

"Sh! not so loud: he'll hear you," Mary said.

"I want him to: he'll have to soon or late."

"He's worn out. He's asleep beside the stove.

97

When I came up from Rowe's I found him here,
Huddled against the barn door fast asleep.
A miserable sight, and frightening, too—
You needn't smile—I didn't recognize him—
I wasn't looking for him—and he's changed.
Wait till you see."

"Where did you say he'd been?"

"He didn't say. I dragged him to the house.
And gave him tea and tried to make him smoke.
I tried to make him talk about his travels.
Nothing would do; he just kept nodding off."

"What did he say? Did he say anything?"

"But little."

"Anything? Mary, confess
He said he'd come to ditch the meadow for me."

"Warren!"
"But did he? I just want to know."

"Of course he did. What would you have him say?
Surely you wouldn't grudge the poor old man
Some humble way to save his self-respect.
He added, if you really care to know,
He meant to clear the upper pasture, too.
That sounds like something you have heard before?
Warren, I wish you could have heard the way
He jumbled everything. I stopped to look
Two or three times—he made me feel so queer—
To see if he was talking in his sleep.
He ran on Harold Wilson—you remember—
The boy you had in haying four years since.
He's finished school, and teaching in his college.
Silas declares you'll have to get him back.
He says they two will make a team for work:
Between them they will lay this farm as smooth!
The way he mixed that in with other things.
He thinks young Wilson a likely lad, though daft
On education—you know how they fought

All through July under the blazing sun,
Silas up on the cart to build the load,
Harold along beside to pitch it on."

"Yes, I took care to keep well out of earshot."

"Well, those days trouble Silas like a dream.
You wouldn't think they would. How such things linger!
Harold's young college-boy's assurance piqued him.
After so many years he still keeps finding
Good arguments he sees he might have used.
I sympathize. I know just how it feels
To think of the right thing to say too late.
Harold's associated in his mind with Latin.
He asked me what I thought of Harold's saying
He studied Latin, like the violin,
Because he liked it—that an argument!
He said he couldn't make the boy believe
He could find water with a hazel prong—
Which showed how much good school had ever done him.
He wanted to go over that. But most of all
He thinks if he could have another chance
To teach him how to build a load of hay—"

"I know, that's Silas' one accomplishment
He bundles every forkful in its place,
And tags and numbers it for future reference,
So he can find and easily dislodge it
In the unloading. Silas does that well.
He takes it out in bunches like big birds' nests.
You never see him standing on the hay
He's trying to lift, straining to lift himself."

"He thinks if he could teach him that, he'd be
Some good perhaps to someone in the world.
He hates to see a boy the fool of books.
Poor Silas, so concerned for other folk,
And nothing to look backward to with pride,
And nothing to look forward to with hope.
So now and never any different."

Part of a moon was falling down the west,
Dragging the whole sky with it to the hills

Its light poured softly in her lap. She saw it
And spread her apron to it. She put out her hand
Among the harplike morning-glory strings,
Taut with the dew from garden bed to eaves,
As if she played unheard some tenderness
That wrought on him beside her in the night.
"Warren," she said, "he has come home to die:
You needn't be afraid he'll leave you this time."

"Home," he mocked gently.

                "Yes, what else but home?

It all depends on what you mean by home.
Of course he's nothing to us, any more
Than was the hound that came a stranger to us
Out of the woods, worn out upon the trail."

"Home is the place where, when you have to go there,
They have to take you in."

                    "I should have called it
Something you somehow haven't to deserve."

Warren leaned out and took a step or two,
Picked up a little stick, and brought it back
And broke it in his hand and tossed it by.
"Silas has better claim on us you think
Than on his brother? Thirteen little miles
As the road winds would bring him to his door.
Silas has walked that far no doubt today.
Why doesn't he go there? His brother's rich,
A somebody—director in the bank."

"He never told us that."

              "We know it, though."

"I think his brother ought to help, of course.
I'll see to that if there is need. He ought of right
To take him in, and might be willing to—
He may be better than appearances.

But have some pity on Silas. Do you think
If he had any pride in claiming kin
Or anything he looked for from his brother,
He'd keep so still about him all this time?"
"I wonder what's between them."

                    "I can tell you.
Silas is what he is—we wouldn't mind him—
But just the kind that kinsfolk can't abide.
He never did a thing so very bad.
He don't know why he isn't quite as good
As anybody. Worthless though he is,
He won't be made ashamed to please his brother."

"*I* can't think Si ever hurt anyone."

"No, but he hurt my heart the way he lay
And rolled his old head on that sharp-edged chair-back.
He wouldn't let me put him on the lounge.
You must go in and see what you can do.
I made the bed up for him there tonight.
You'll be surprised at him—how much he's broken.
His working days are done; I'm sure of it."

"I'd not be in a hurry to say that."

"I haven't been. Go, look, see for yourself.
But, Warren, please remember how it is:
He's come to help you ditch the meadow.
He has a plan. You mustn't laugh at him.
He may not speak of it, and then he may.
I'll sit and see if that small sailing cloud
Will hit or miss the moon."

                    It hit the moon.
Then there were three there, making a dim row,
The moon, the little silver cloud, and she.

Warren returned—too soon, it seemed to her—
Slipped to her side, caught up her hand and waited.

"Warren?" she questioned.
                    "Dead," was all he answered.

The Overcoat

Nikolai Gogol

Translated by Andrew R. MacAndrew

ONCE, in a department . . . but better not mention which department. There is nothing touchier than departments, regiments, bureaus, in fact, any caste of officials. Things have reached the point where every individual takes an insult to himself as a slur on society as a whole. It seems that not long ago a complaint was lodged by the police inspector of I forget which town, in which he stated clearly that government institutions had been imperiled and his own sacred name taken in vain. In evidence he produced a huge volume, practically a novel, in which, every ten pages, a police inspector appears, and what's more, at times completely drunk. So, to stay out of trouble, let us refer to it just as *a department.*

And so, once, in *a department,* there worked a clerk. This clerk was nothing much to speak of: he was small, somewhat pockmarked, his hair was somewhat reddish and he even looked somewhat blind. Moreover, he was getting thin on top, had wrinkled cheeks and a complexion that might be aptly described as hemorrhoidal. But that's the Petersburg climate for you.

As to his civil-service category (for first a man's standing should be established), he was what is called an eternal penpusher, a lowly ninth-class clerk, the usual butt of the jeers and jokes of those writers who have the congenial habit of biting those who cannot bite back.

The clerk's name was Shoenik. There is no doubt that this name derives from shoe but we know nothing of how, why, or when. His father, his grandfather, and even his brother-in-law wore boots, having new soles put on them not more than three times a year.

His first name was Akaky, like his father's, which made him Akaky Akakievich. This may sound somewhat strange and contrived but it is not contrived at all, and, in view of the circumstances, any other name was unthinkable. If I am not mistaken, Akaky Akakievich was born on the night between the 22nd and the 23rd of March. His late mother, an excellent woman and the wife of a clerk, had made all the arrangements for the child's christening, and, while she was still confined to her bed, the godparents arrived: the worthy Ivan Yeroshkin, head clerk in the Senate, and Arina Whitetumkin, the wife of a police captain, a woman of rare virtue.

The new mother was given her pick of the following three names for her son: Mochius, Sossius, and that of the martyr, Hotzazat. "That won't do," Akaky's late mother thought. "Those names are . . . how shall I put it . . ." To please her, the godparents opened the calendar at another page and again three names came out: Strifilius, Dulius, and Varachasius.

"We're in a mess," the old woman said. "Who ever heard of such names? If it was something like Varadat or Varuch, I wouldn't object . . . but Strifilius and Varachasius . . ."

So they turned to yet another page and out came Pavsicachius and Vachtisius.

"Well, that's that," the mother said. "That settles it. He'll just have to be Akaky like his father."

So that's how Akaky Akakievich originated.

And when they christened the child it cried and twisted its features into a sour expression as though it had a foreboding that it would become a ninth-class clerk.

Well, that's how it all happened and it has been reported here just to show that the child couldn't have been called anything but Akaky.

No one remembers who helped him get his appointment to the department or when he started working there. Directors and all sorts of chiefs came and went but he was always to be found at the same place, in the same position, and in the same capacity, that of copying clerk. Until, after a while, people began to believe that he must have been born just as he was, shabby frock coat, bald patch, and all.

In the office, not the slightest respect was shown him. The porters didn't get up when he passed. In fact, they didn't even raise their eyes, as if nothing but an ordinary fly had passed through the reception room. His chiefs were cold and despotic with him. Some head clerks would just thrust a paper under his nose without even saying, "Copy this," or "Here's a nice interesting little job for you," or some such pleasant remark as is current in well-bred offices. And Akaky Akakievich would take the paper without glancing up to see who had put it under his nose or whether the person was entitled to do so. And right away he would set about copying it.

The young clerks laughed at him and played tricks on him to the limit of their clerkish wit. They made up stories about him and told them in front of him. They said that his seventy-year-old landlady beat him and asked him when the wedding would be. They scattered scraps of paper which they said was snow over his head. But with all this going on, Akaky Akakievich never said a word and even acted as though no one were there. It didn't even affect his work and in spite of their loud badgering he made no mistakes in his copying. Only when they tormented him unbearably, when they jogged his elbow and prevented him from getting on with his work, would he say:

"Let me be. Why do you do this to me? . . ."

And his words and the way he said them sounded strange. There was something touching about them. Once a young man who was new to the office started to tease him, following the crowd. Suddenly he stopped as if awakened from a trance and, after that, he couldn't stand the others, whom at first he had deemed decent people. And for a long time to come, during his gayest moments, he would suddenly see in his mind's eye the little, balding clerk and he would hear the words, "Let me be. Why do you do this to me?" and within those words rang the phrase, "I am your brother." And the young man would cover his face with his hands. Later in life, he often shuddered, musing about the wickedness of man toward man and all the cruelty and vulgarity which are concealed under refined manners. And this, he decided, was also true of men who were considered upright and honorable.

It would be hard to find a man who so lived for his job. It would not be enough to say that he worked conscientiously—he worked with love. There, in his copying, he found an interesting, pleasant world for himself and his delight was reflected in his face. He had his favorites among the letters of the alphabet and, when he came to them, he would chuckle, wink and help them along with his lips so that they could almost be read on his face as they were formed by his pen.

Had he been rewarded in proportion with his zeal, he would, perhaps to his own surprise, have been promoted to fifth-class clerk. But all he got out of it was, as his witty colleagues put it, a pin for his buttonhole and hemorrhoids to sit on.

Still, it would be unfair to say that no attention had ever been paid him. One of the successive directors, a kindly man, who thought Akaky Akakievich should be rewarded for his long service, suggested that he be given something more interesting than ordinary copying. So he was asked to prepare an already drawn-up document for referral to another department. Actually, all he had to do was to give it a new heading and change some of the verbs from the first to the third person. But Akaky Akakievich found this work so complicated that he broke into a sweat and finally, mopping his brow, he said:

"Oh no, I would rather have something to copy instead."

After that they left him to his copying forever. And aside from it, it seemed, nothing existed for him.

He never gave a thought to his clothes. His frock coat, which was supposed to be green, had turned a sort of mealy reddish. Its collar was very low and very narrow so that his neck, which was really quite ordinary, looked incredibly long—like the spring necks of the head-shaking plaster kittens which foreign peddlers carry around on their heads on trays. And, somehow, there was always something stuck to Akaky Akakievich's frock coat, a wisp of hay, a little thread. Then too, he had a knack of passing under windows just when refuse happened to be thrown out and as a result was forever carrying around on his hat melon rinds and other such rubbish.

Never did he pay any attention to what was going on around him in the street. In this he was very different from the other members of the pen-pushing brotherhood, who are so keen-eyed and observant that they'll notice an undone strap on the bottom of someone's trousers, an observation that unfailingly molds their features into a sly sneer. But even when Akaky Akakievich's eyes were resting on something, he saw superimposed on it his own well-formed, neat handwriting. Perhaps it was only when, out of nowhere, a horse rested its head on his shoulder and sent a blast of wind down his cheek that he'd realized he was not in the middle of a line but in the middle of a street.

When he got home he would sit straight down to the table and quickly gulp his cabbage soup, followed by beef and onions. He never noticed the taste and ate it with flies and whatever else God happened to send along. When his stomach began to feel bloated, he would get up from the table, take out his inkwell, and copy papers he had brought with him from the office. And if there weren't any papers to copy for the office, he would make a copy for his own pleasure, especially if the document were unusual. Unusual, not for the beauty of its style, but because it was addressed to some new or important personage.

Even during those hours when light has completely disappeared from the gray Petersburg sky and the pen-pushing brotherhood have filled themselves with dinner of one sort or another, each as best he can according to his income and his preference; when everyone has rested from the scraping of pens in the office, from running around on their own and others' errands; when the restless human being has relaxed after the tasks, sometimes unnecessary, he sets himself; and the clerks hasten to give over the remaining hours to pleasure—the more enterprising among them rushes to the theater, another walks in the streets, allotting his time to the inspection of ladies' hats; another spends his evening paying compliments to some prettyish damsel, the queen of a small circle of clerks; another, the most frequent case, goes to visit a brother clerk, who lives somewhere on the third or fourth floor, in two small rooms with a hall of a kitchen and some little pretensions to fashion, a lamp or some other article bought at great sacrifice, such as going without dinner or outside pleasures—in brief, at the time when all clerks have dispersed among the lodgings of their friends to play a little game of whist, sipping tea from glasses and nibbling biscuits, inhaling the smoke from their long pipes, relaying, while the cards are dealt, some bit of gossip that has trickled down from high society, a thing which a Russian cannot do without whatever his circumstances, and even, when there's nothing else to talk about, telling once again the ancient joke about the commandant to whom it was reported that someone had hacked the tail off the horse of the monument to Peter the First—in a word, when everyone else was trying to have a good time, Akaky Akakievich was not even thinking of diverting himself.

No one had ever seen him at a party in the evening. Having written to his heart's content, he would go to bed, smiling in anticipation of the morrow, of what God would send him to copy.

Thus flowed the life of a man who, on a yearly salary of four hundred rubles, was content with his lot. And perhaps it would have flowed on to old age if it hadn't been for the various disasters which are scattered along life's paths, not only for ninth-class clerks, but even for eighth-, seventh-, sixth-class clerks and all the way up to State Councilors, Privy Councilors, and even to those who counsel no one, not even themselves.

In Petersburg, there's a formidable enemy for all those who receive a salary in the neighborhood of four hundred rubles a year. The enemy is none other than our northern cold, although they say it's very healthy.

Between eight and nine in the morning, at just the time when the streets are filled with people walking to their offices, the cold starts to mete out indiscriminately such hard, stinging flicks on noses that the wretched clerks don't know where to put them. And when the cold pinches the brows and brings tears to the eyes of those in high positions, ninth-class clerks are completely defenseless. They can only wrap themselves in their threadbare overcoats and run as fast as they can the five or six blocks to the office. Once arrived, they have to stamp their feet in the vestibule until their abilities and talents, which have been frozen on the way, thaw out once again.

Akaky Akakievich had noticed that for some time the cold had been attacking his back and shoulders quite viciously, try as he might to sprint the prescribed distance. He finally began to wonder whether the fault did not lie with his overcoat. When he gave it a good looking-over in his room, he discovered that in two or three places—the shoulders and back—it had become very much like gauze. The cloth was worn so thin that it let the draft in, and, to make things worse, the lining had disintegrated.

It must be noted that Akaky Akakievich's overcoat had also been a butt of the clerk's jokes. They had even deprived it of its respectable name, referring to it as the old dressing gown. And, as far as that goes, it did have a strange shape. Its collar shrank with every year, since it was used to patch other areas. And the patching, which did not flatter the tailor, made the overcoat baggy and ugly.

Having located the trouble, Akaky Akakievich decided to take the cloak to Petrovich, a tailor who lived somewhere on the fourth floor, up a back stairs, and who, one-eyed and pockmarked as he was, was still quite good at repairing clerks' and other such people's trousers and frock coats, provided he happened to be sober and hadn't other things on his mind.

We shouldn't, of course, waste too many words on the tailor, but since it has become the fashion to give a thorough description of every character figuring in a story, there's nothing to be done but to give you Petrovich.

At first he was called just Grigory and was the serf of some gentleman or other. He began to call himself Petrovich when he received his freedom and took to drinking rather heavily on all holidays, on the big ones at first and then, without distinction, on all church holidays—on any day marked by a little cross on the calendar. In this he was true to the traditions of his forefathers, and, when his wife nagged him about it, he called her impious and a German. Now that we've mentioned his wife, we'd better say a word or two about her, too. But unfortunately very little is known about her, except that Petrovich had a wife who wore a bonnet instead of a kerchief, but was apparently no beauty, since, on meeting her, it occurred to no one but an occasional soldier to peek under that bonnet of hers, twitching his mustache and making gurgling sounds.

Going up the stairs leading to Petrovich's place, which, to be honest about it, were saturated with water and slops and exuded that ammonia smell which burns your eyes and which you'll always find on the back stairs of all Petersburg houses— going up those stairs, Akaky Akakievich was already conjecturing how much Petrovich would ask and making up his mind not to pay more than two rubles.

The door stood open because Petrovich's wife was cooking some fish or other and had made so much smoke in the kitchen that you couldn't even see the cockroaches. Akaky Akakievich went through the kitchen without even seeing Mrs. Petrovich and finally reached the other room, where he saw Petrovich sitting on a wide, unpainted wooden table, with his legs crossed under him like a Turkish pasha.

He was barefoot, as tailors at work usually are, and the first thing Akaky Akakievich saw was Petrovich's big toe, with its twisted nail, thick and hard like a tortoise shell. A skein of silk and cotton thread hung around Petrovich's neck. On his knees there was some old garment. For the past three minutes he had been trying to thread his needle, very irritated at the darkness of the room and even with the thread itself, muttering under his breath: "It won't go through, the pig, it's killing me, the bitch!" Akaky Akakievich was unhappy to find Petrovich so irritated. He preferred to negotiate when the tailor was a little under the weather, or, as his wife put it, "when the one-eyed buzzard had a load on." When caught in such a state, Petrovich usually gave way very readily on the price and would even thank Akaky Akakievich with respectful bows and all that. True, afterwards, his wife would come whining that her husband had charged too little because he was drunk; but all you had to do was add ten kopeks and it was a deal.

This time, however, Petrovich seemed to be sober and therefore curt, intractable, and likely to charge an outrageous price.

Akaky Akakievich realized this and would have liked to beat a hasty retreat, but the die was cast. Petrovich had fixed his one eye on him and Akaky Akakievich involuntarily came out with:

"Hello, Petrovich."

"Wish you good day, sir," said Petrovich and bent his eye toward Akaky Akakievich's hands to see what kind of spoil he had brought him.

"Well, Petrovich, I've come . . . see . . . the thing is . . . to . . ."

It should be realized that Akaky Akakievich used all sorts of prepositions, adverbs and all those meaningless little parts of speech when he spoke. Moreover, if the matter were very involved, he generally didn't finish his sentences and opened them with the words: "This, really, is absolutely, I mean to say . . ." and then nothing more—he had forgotten that he hadn't said what he wanted to.

"What is it then?" Petrovich asked, looking over Akaky Akakievich's frock coat with his one eye, the collar, the sleeves, the back, the tails, the buttonholes, all of which he was already acquainted with, since, repairs and all, it was his own work. That's just what tailors do as soon as they see you.

"Well, it's like this, Petrovich . . . my cloak, well, the material . . . look, you can see, everywhere else it's very strong, well, it's a bit dusty and it looks rather shabby, but it's not really . . . look, it's just in one place it's a little . . . on the back here, and here too . . . it's a little worn . . . and here on this shoulder too, a little—and that's all. There's not much work . . ."

Petrovich took Akaky Akakievich's old dressing gown, as his colleagues called it, spread it out on the table and looked it over at length. Then he shook his head and, stretching out his hand, took from the windowsill a snuffbox embellished with the portrait of a general, though just what general it was impossible to tell since right where his face used to be there was now a dent glued over with a piece of paper. Taking some snuff, Petrovich spread the overcoat out on his hands, held it up against the light and again shook his head. Then he turned the overcoat inside out, with the lining up, and shook his head again. Then, once more, he removed the snuffbox lid with its general under the piece of paper, and, stuffing snuff into his nose, closed the box, put it away, and finally said:

"No. It can't be mended. It's no use."

At these words, Akaky Akakievich's heart turned over.

"But why can't it be, Petrovich?" he said in the imploring voice of a child. "Look, the only trouble is that it's worn around the shoulders. I'm sure you have some scraps of cloth . . ."

"As for scraps, I suppose I could find them," Petrovich said, "but I couldn't sew them on. The whole thing is rotten. It'd go to pieces the moment you touched it with a needle."

"Well, if it starts to go, you'll catch it with a patch . . ."

"But there's nothing for patches to hold to. It's too far gone. It's only cloth in name—a puff of wind and it'll disintegrate."

"Still, I'm sure you can make them hold just the same. Otherwise, really, Petrovich, see what I mean . . ."

"No," Petrovich said with finality, "nothing can be done with it. It's just no good. You'd better make yourself some bands out of it to wrap round your legs when it's cold and socks aren't enough to keep you warm. The Germans thought up those things to make money for themselves."—Petrovich liked to take a dig at the Germans whenever there was a chance.—"As to the overcoat, it looks as if you'll have to have a new one made."

At the word "new" Akaky Akakievich's vision became foggy and the whole room began to sway. The only thing he saw clearly was the general with the paper-covered face on the lid of Petrovich's snuffbox.

"What do you mean a *new* one?" he said, talking as if in a dream. "I haven't even got the money . . ."

"A new one," Petrovich repeated with savage calm.

"Well, but if I really had to have a new one, how would it be that . . ."

"That is, what will it cost?"

"Yes."

"Well, it will be over one hundred and fifty rubles," Petrovich said, pursing his lips meaningfully. He liked strong effects, he liked to perplex someone suddenly and then observe the grimace that his words produced.

"A hundred and fifty rubles for an overcoat!" shrieked the poor Akaky Akakievich, shrieked perhaps for the first time in his life, since he was always noted for his quietness.

"Yes, sir," said Petrovich, "but what an overcoat! And if it is to have marten on the collar and a silk-lined hood, that'll bring it up to two hundred."

"Please, Petrovich, please," Akaky Akakievich said beseechingly, not taking in Petrovich's words or noticing his dramatic effects, "mend it somehow, just enough to make it last a little longer."

"No sir, it won't work. It would be a waste of labor and money."

Akaky Akakievich left completely crushed. And when he left, Petrovich, instead of going back to his work, remained for a long time immobile, his lips pursed meaningfully. He was pleased with himself for having upheld his own honor as well as that of the entire tailoring profession.

Akaky Akakievich emerged into the street feeling as if he were in a dream. "So that's it," he repeated to himself. "I never suspected it would turn out this way . . ." and then, after a brief pause, he went on: "So that's it! Here's how it turns out in the end, and I, really, simply couldn't have foreseen it." After another, longer pause, he added: "And so here we are! Here's how things stand. I in no way expected . . . but this is impossible . . . what a business!" Muttering thus, instead of going home, he went in the opposite direction, without having the slightest idea of what was going on.

As he was walking, a chimney sweep brushed his dirty side against him and blackened his whole shoulder; a whole bucketful of lime was showered over him from the top of a house under construction. But he noticed nothing and only when he bumped into a watchman who, resting his halberd near him, was shaking some snuff out of a horn into his calloused palm, did he come to a little and that only because the watchman said:

"Ya hafta knock my head off? Ya got the whole sidewalk, ain'tcha?"

This caused him to look about him and turn back toward home. Only then did he start to collect his thoughts and to see his real position clearly. He began to talk to himself, not in bits of phrases now but sensibly, as to a wise friend in whom he could confide.

"Oh no," he said, "that wasn't the moment to speak to Petrovich. Right now he's sort of . . . his wife obviously has given him a beating . . . that sort of thing. It'd be better if I went and saw him Sunday morning. After Saturday night, his one eye will be wandering and he'll be tired and in need of another drink, and his wife won't give him the money. So I'll slip him a quarter and that will make him more reasonable and so, for the overcoat . . ." Thus Akaky Akakievich tried to reassure himself, and persuaded himself to wait for Sunday.

When that day came, he waited at a distance until he saw Petrovich's wife leave the house and then went up. After his Saturday night libations, Petrovich's eye certainly was wandering. He hung his head and looked terribly sleepy. But, despite all that, as soon as he learned what Akaky Akakievich had come about, it was if the devil had poked him.

"It can't be done," he said. "You must order a new one."

Here Akaky Akakievich pressed the quarter on him.

"Thank you," Petrovich said. "I'll drink a short one to you, sir. And as to the overcoat, you can stop worrying. It's worthless. But I'll make you a first-rate new one. That I'll see to."

Akaky Akakievich tried once more to bring the conversation around to mending, but Petrovich, instead of listening, said:

"I'll make you a new one, sir, and you can count on me to do my best. I may even make the collar fastened with silver-plated clasps for you."

At this point Akaky Akakievich saw that he'd have to have a new overcoat and he became utterly depressed. Where was he going to get the money? There was of course the next holiday bonus. But the sum involved had long ago been allotted to other needs. He had to order new trousers, to pay the cobbler for replacing the tops of his boots. He owed the seamstress for three shirts and simply had to have two items of underwear which one cannot refer to in print. In fact, all the money, to the last kopek, was owed, and even if the director made an unexpectedly generous gesture and allotted him, instead of forty rubles, a whole forty-five or even fifty, the difference would be a drop in the ocean in the overcoat outlay.

It is true Akaky Akakievich knew that, on occasions, Petrovich slapped on heaven knows what exorbitant price, so that even his wife couldn't refrain from exclaiming:

"Have you gone mad, you fool! One day he accepts work for nothing, and the next, something gets into him and makes him ask for more than he's worth himself."

But he also knew that Petrovich would agree to make him a new overcoat for eighty rubles. Even so, where was he to find the eighty? He could perhaps scrape together half that sum. Even a little more. But where would he get the other half? . . . Let us, however, start with the first half and see where it was to come from.

Akaky Akakievich had a rule: whenever he spent one ruble, he slipped a copper into a little box with a slot in its side. Every six months, he counted the coppers and changed them for silver. He'd been doing this for a long time and, after all these years, had accumulated more than forty rubles. So this came to one half. But what about the remaining forty rubles?

Akaky Akakievich thought and thought and decided that he would have to reduce his regular expenses for an entire year at least. It would mean going without his evening tea; not burning candles at night, and, if he absolutely had to have light, going to his landlady's room and working by her candle. It would mean, when walking in the street, stepping as carefully as possible over the cobbles and paving stones, almost tiptoeing, so as not to wear out the soles of his boots too rapidly, and giving out his laundry as seldom as possible, and, so that it shouldn't get too soiled, undressing as soon as he got home and staying in just his thin cotton dressing gown, which, if time hadn't taken pity on it, would itself have collapsed long ago.

It must be admitted that, at first, he suffered somewhat from these restrictions. But then he became accustomed to them somehow and things went smoothly again. He even got used to going hungry in the evenings, but then he was able to feed himself spiritually, carrying within him the eternal idea of his overcoat-to-be. It was as if his existence had become somehow fuller, as if he had married and another human being were there with him, as if he were no longer alone on life's road but walking by the side of a delightful companion. And that companion was none other than the overcoat itself, with its thick padding and strong lining that would last forever. In some way, he became more alive, even stronger-minded, like a man who has determined his ultimate goal in life.

From his face and actions all the marks of vacillation and indecision vanished.

At times, there was even a fire in his eyes and the boldest, wildest notions flashed through his head—perhaps he should really consider having marten put on the collar? The intensity of these thoughts almost distracted his attention from his work. Once he almost made a mistake, which caused him to exclaim— true, very softly—"Oof!" and to cross himself.

At least once each month he looked in on Petrovich to discuss the overcoat—the best place to buy the material, its color, its price . . . Then, on the way home, a little worried but always pleased, he mused about how, finally, all this buying would be over and the coat would be made.

Things went ahead faster than he had expected. Beyond all expectations, the director granted Akaky Akakievich not forty, nor forty-five, but a whole sixty rubles. Could he have had a premonition that Akaky Akakievich needed a new overcoat, or had it just happened by itself? Whatever it was, Akaky Akakievich wound up with an extra twenty rubles. This circumstance speeded matters up. Another two or three months of moderate hunger and he had almost all of the eighty rubles he needed. His heartbeat, generally very quiet, grew faster.

As soon as he could, he set out for the store with Petrovich. They bought excellent material, which is not surprising since they had been planning the move for all of six months, and a month had seldom gone by without Akaky Akakievich dropping into the shop to work out prices. Petrovich himself said that there was no better material to be had.

For the lining they chose calico, but so good and thick that, Petrovich said, it even looked better and glossier than silk. They did not buy marten because it was too expensive. Instead they got cat, the best available—cat which at a distance could always be taken for marten. Petrovich spent two full weeks on the overcoat because of all the quilting he had to do. He charged twelve rubles for his work—it was impossible to take less; it had been sewn with silk, with fine double seams, and Petrovich had gone over each seam again afterwards with his own teeth, squeezing out different patterns with them.

It was—well, it's hard to say exactly which day it was, but it was probably the most solemn day in Akaky Akakievich's life, the day Petrovich finally brought him the overcoat. He brought it in the morning, just before it was time to go to the office. There couldn't have been a better moment for the coat to arrive, because cold spells had been creeping in and threatened to become even more severe. Petrovich appeared with the coat, as befits a good tailor. He had an expression of importance on his face that Akaky Akakievich had never seen before. He looked very much aware of having performed an important act, an act that carries tailors over the chasm which separates those who merely put in linings and do repairs from those who create.

He took the overcoat out of the gigantic handkerchief—just fresh from the wash—in which he had wrapped it to deliver it. The handkerchief he folded neatly and put in his pocket, ready for use. Then he took the coat, looked at it with great pride and, holding it in both hands threw it quite deftly around Akaky Akakievich's shoulders. He pulled and smoothed it down at the back, wrapped it around Akaky Akakievich, leaving it a little open at the front. Akaky Akakievich, a down-to-earth sort of man, wanted to try out the sleeves. Petrovich helped him to pull his arms through and it turned out that with the sleeves too it was good. In a word, it was clear that the coat fitted perfectly.

Petrovich didn't fail to take advantage of the occasion to remark that it was only because he did without a signboard, lived in a small side street, and had known Akaky Akakievich for a long time that he had charged him so little. On Nevsky Avenue, nowadays, he said, they'd have taken seventy-five rubles for the work alone. Akaky Akakievich had no desire to debate the point with Petrovich—he was always rather awed by the big sums which Petrovich liked to mention to impress people. He paid up, thanked Petrovich, and left for the office wearing his new overcoat.

Petrovich followed him and stood for a long time in the street, gazing at the overcoat from a distance. Then he plunged into a curving side street, took a shortcut, and reemerged on the street ahead of Akaky Akakievich, so that he could have another look at the coat from another angle.

Meanwhile, Akaky Akakievich walked on, bubbling with good spirits. Every second of every minute he felt the new overcoat on his shoulders and several times he even let out a little chuckle of inward pleasure. Indeed, the overcoat presented him with a double advantage: it was warm and it was good. He didn't notice his trip at all and suddenly found himself before the office building. In the porter's lodge, he slipped off the overcoat, inspected it, and entrusted it to the porter's special care.

No one knows how, but it suddenly became general knowledge in the office that Akaky Akakievich had a new overcoat and that the old dressing gown no longer existed. Elbowing one another, they all rushed to the cloakroom to see the new coat. Then they proceeded to congratulate him. He smiled at first, but then the congratulations became too exuberant, and he felt embarrassed. And when they surrounded him and started trying to persuade him that the very least he could do was to invite them over one evening to drink to the coat, Akaky Akakievich felt completely at a loss, didn't know what to do with himself, what to say or how to talk himself out of it. And a few minutes later, all red in the face, he was trying rather naively to convince them that it wasn't a new overcoat at all, that it wasn't much, that it was an old one.

In the end, a clerk, no lesser person than an assistant to the head clerk, probably wanting to show that he wasn't too proud to mingle with those beneath him, said:

"All right then, I'll do it instead of Akaky Akakievich. I invite you all over for a party. Come over to my place tonight. Incidentally, it happens to be my birthday today."

Naturally the clerks now congratulated the head clerk's assistant and happily accepted his invitation. Akaky Akakievich started to excuse himself, but he was told that it would be rude on his part, a disgrace, so he had to give way in the end. And later he was even rather pleased that he had accepted, since it would give him an opportunity to wear the new coat in the evening too.

Akaky Akakievich felt as if it were a holiday. He arrived home in the happiest frame of mind, took off the overcoat, hung it up very carefully on the wall, gave the material and the lining one more admiring inspection. Then he took out that ragged item known as the old dressing gown and put it next to the new overcoat, looked at it and began to laugh, so great was the difference between the two. And long after that, while eating dinner, he snorted every time he thought of the dressing gown. He felt very gay during his dinner, and afterwards he did no copying whatsoever. Instead he wallowed in luxury for a while, lying on his bed until dark. Then, without further dallying, he dressed, pulled on his new overcoat and went out.

It is, alas, impossible to say just where the party-giving clerk lived. My memory is beginning to fail me badly and everything in Petersburg, streets and houses, has become so mixed up in my head that it's very difficult to extract anything from it and to present it in an orderly fashion. Be that as it may, it is a fact that the clerk in question lived in a better district of the city, which means not too close to Akaky Akakievich.

To start with, Akaky Akakievich had to pass through a maze of deserted, dimly lit streets, but, toward the clerk's house, the streets became lighter and livelier. More pedestrians began flashing by more often; there were some well-dressed ladies and men with beaver collars. And, instead of the drivers with their wooden, fretworked sledges studded with gilt nails, he came across smart coachmen in crimson velvet caps, in lacquered sledges, with bearskin lap rugs. He even saw some carriages darting past with decorated boxes, their wheels squeaking on the snow.

Akaky Akakievich gazed around him. For several years now he hadn't been out in the evening. He stopped before the small, lighted window of a shop, staring curiously at a picture of a pretty woman kicking off her shoe and thereby showing her whole leg, which was not bad at all; in the background, some man or other with side whiskers and a handsome Spanish goatee was sticking his head through a door leading to another room. Akaky Akakievich shook his head, snorted, smiled and walked on. Why did he snort? Was it because he had come across something that, although completely strange to him, still aroused in him, as it would in anyone, a certain instinct—or did he think, as many clerks do, along the following lines: "Well, really, the French! If they are after something . . . that sort of thing . . . then, really! . . ." Maybe he didn't even think that. After all, one can't just creep into a man's soul and find out everything he's thinking.

At last he reached the house in which the head clerk's assistant lived. And he lived in style, on the second floor, with the staircase lighted by a lantern. In the hall, Akaky Akakievich found several rows of galoshes. Amidst the galoshes, a samovar was hissing and puffing steam. All around the walls hung overcoats and cloaks, some with beaver collars and others with velvet lapels. The noise and talk that could be heard through the partition became suddenly clear and resounding when the door opened and a servant came out with a tray of empty glasses, a cream jug, and a basket of cookies. It was clear that the clerks had arrived long before and had already drunk their first round of tea.

Akaky Akakievich hung his coat up and went in. In a flash, he took in the candles, the clerks, the pipes, the card tables, while his ears were filled with the hubbub of voices rising all around him and the banging of chairs being moved. Awkwardly, he paused in the middle of the room, trying to think what to do. But he had been noticed and his arrival was greeted with a huge yell. Immediately everybody rushed out into the hall to have another look at his new overcoat. Akaky Akakievich felt a bit confused, but, being an uncomplicated man, he was rather pleased when everyone agreed that it was a good overcoat.

Soon, however, they abandoned him and his overcoat and turned their attention, as was to be expected, to the card tables.

The din, the voices, the presence of so many people—all this was unreal to Akaky Akakievich. He had no idea how to behave, where to put his hands, his feet, or, for that matter, his whole body. He sat down near a card table, stared at the cards and peeked in turn into the faces of the players. In a little while he got bored and began to yawn, feeling rather sleepy—it was long past his usual bedtime. He wanted to take leave of the host, but they wouldn't let him go. He really had to toast his new overcoat with champagne, they insisted. They made Akaky Akakievich drink two glasses of champagne, after which he felt that the party was becoming gayer, but nevertheless he was quite unable to forget that it was now midnight and that he should have gone home long ago.

In spite of everything his host could think up to keep him, he went quietly out into the hall, found his overcoat, which to his annoyance was lying on the floor, shook it, carefully removed every speck he could find on it, put it on and walked down the stairs and out into the street.

The street was still lighted. Some little stores, those meeting places for servants and people of every sort, were open, while others, although closed, still showed a long streak of light under their doors, which indicated that the company had not yet dispersed and that the menservants and maids were finishing up their gossip and their conversations, leaving their masters perplexed as to their whereabouts.

Akaky Akakievich walked along in such a gay mood that, who knows why, he almost darted after a lady who flashed by him like a streak of lightning, every part of her body astir with independent, fascinating motion. Still, he restrained himself immediately, went back to walking slowly and even wondered where that compulsion to gallop had come from.

Soon there stretched out before him those deserted streets which, even in the daytime, are not so gay, and, now that it was night, looked even more desolate. Fewer street lamps were lit—obviously a smaller oil allowance was given out in this district. Then came wooden houses and fences; not a soul around, nothing but glistening snow and the black silhouettes of the low, sleeping hovels with their shuttered windows. He came to the spot where the street cut through a square so immense that the houses opposite were hardly visible beyond its sinister emptiness.

God knows where, far away on the edge of the world, he could see the glow of a brazier by a watchman's hut.

Akaky Akakievich's gay mood definitely waned. He could not suppress a shiver as he stepped out into the square, a foreboding of evil in his heart. He glanced behind him and to either side—it was like being in the middle of the sea. "No, it's better not to look," he thought, and walked on with his eyes shut. And when he opened them again to see if the other side of the square was close, he saw instead, standing there, almost in front of his nose, people with mustaches, although he couldn't make out, exactly who or what. Then his vision became foggy and there was a beating in his chest.

"Why, there's my overcoat," one of the people thundered, grabbing him by the collar.

Akaky Akakievich was just going to shout out "Help!" when another brought a fist about the size of a clerk's head up to his very mouth, and said:

"You just try and yell . . ."

Akaky Akakievich felt them pull off his coat, then he received a knee in the groin. He went down on his back and after that he lay in the snow and felt nothing more.

When he came to a few minutes later and scrambled to his feet, there was no one around. He felt cold and, when he realized that the overcoat was gone, desperate. He let out a yell. But his voice didn't come close to reaching the other side of the square.

Frantic, he hollered all the way across the square as he scrambled straight toward the watchman's hut. The watchman was standing beside it, leaning on his halberd, and gazing out across the square, wondering who it could be running toward him and shouting. At last Akaky Akakievich reached him. Gasping for breath, he began shouting at him—what sort of a watchman did he think he was, hadn't he seen anything, and why the devil had he allowed them to rob a man? The watchman said he had seen no one except the two men who had stopped Akaky Akakievich in the middle of the square, who he had thought were friends of his, and that instead of hollering at the watchman, he'd better go and see the police inspector tomorrow and the inspector would find out who had taken the overcoat.

Akaky Akakievich hurried home; he was in a terrible state. The little hair he had left, on his temples and on the back of his head, was completely disheveled, there was snow all down one side of him and on his chest and all over his trousers. His old landlady, hearing his impatient banging on the door, jumped out of bed and, with only one shoe on, ran to open up, clutching her nightgown at the neck, probably out of modesty. When she saw the state Akaky Akakievich was in, she stepped back.

When he told her what had happened, she threw up her hands and said that he should go straight to the borough Police Commissioner, that the local police inspector could not be trusted, that he'd just make promises and give him the runaround. So it was best, she said, to go straight to the borough Commissioner. In fact, she even knew him because Anna, her former Finnish cook, had now got a job as a nanny at his house. And the landlady herself often saw him driving past their house. Moreover, she knew he went to church every Sunday and prayed and at the same time looked cheerful and was obviously a good man. Having heard her advice, Akaky Akakievich trudged off sadly to his room and somehow got through the night, though exactly how must be imagined by those who know how to put themselves in another man's place.

Early the next morning, he went to the borough Commissioner's. But it turned out that he was still asleep. He returned at ten and again was told he was asleep. He went back at eleven and was told that the Commissioner was not home. He tried again during the dinner hour but the secretaries in the reception room would not let him in and wanted to know what business had brought him. For once in his life Akaky Akakievich decided to show some character and told them curtly that he must see the Commissioner personally, that they'd better let him in since he was on official government business, that he would lodge a complaint against them and that then they would see.

The secretaries didn't dare say anything to that and one of them went to call the Commissioner. The Commissioner reacted very strangely to Akaky Akakievich's story of the robbery. Instead of concentrating on the main point, he asked Akaky Akakievich what he had been doing out so late, whether he had stopped off somewhere on his way, hadn't he been to a house of ill repute. Akaky Akakievich became very confused and when he left he wasn't sure whether something would be done about his overcoat or not.

That day he did not go to his office for the first time in his life. The next day he appeared, looking very pale and wearing his old dressing gown, which now seemed shabbier than ever. His account of the theft of his overcoat touched many of the clerks, although, even now, there were some who poked fun at him. They decided on the spot to take up a collection for him but they collected next to nothing because the department employees had already had to donate money for a portrait of the Director and to subscribe to some book or other, on the suggestion of the section chief, who was a friend of the author's. So the sum turned out to be the merest trifle.

Someone, moved by compassion, decided to help Akaky Akakievich by giving him good advice. He told him that he had better not go to his local inspector because, even supposing the inspector wanted to impress his superiors and managed to recover the coat, Akaky Akakievich would still find it difficult to obtain it at the police station unless he could present irrefutable proof of ownership. The best thing was to go through a certain important personage who, by writing and contacting the right people, would set things moving faster. So Akaky Akakievich decided to seek an audience with the important personage.

Even to this day, it is not known exactly what position the important personage held or what his duties consisted of. All we need to know is that this important personage had become important quite recently and that formerly he had been an unimportant person. And even his present position was unimportant compared with other, more important ones. But there is always a category of people for whom somebody who is unimportant to others is an important personage. And the personage in question used various devices to play up his importance: for instance, he made the civil servants of lower categories come out to meet him on the stairs before he'd even reached his office; and a subordinate could not approach him directly but had to go through proper channels. That's the way things are in Holy Russia—everyone tries to ape his superior.

They say that one ninth-class clerk, when he was named section chief in a small office, immediately had a partition put up to make a separate room, which he called the conference room. He stationed an usher at the door who had to open it for all those who came in, although the conference room had hardly enough space for a writing table, even without visitors. The audiences and the manner of our important personage were impressive and stately, but quite uncomplicated. The key to his system was severity. He liked to say: "Severity, severity, severity," and as he uttered the word for the third time, he usually looked very meaningfully into the face of the person he was talking to. True, it was not too clear what need there was for all this severity since the ten-odd employees who made up the whole administrative apparatus of his office were quite frightened enough as it was. Seeing him coming, they would leave their work and stand to attention until he had crossed the room. His usual communication with his inferiors was full of severity and consisted almost entirely of three phrases: "How dare you!" "Who do you think you're talking to?" and "Do you appreciate who I am?" Actually, he was a kindly man, a good friend and obliging, but promotion to a high rank had gone to his head, knocked him completely off balance, and he just didn't know how to act. When he happened to be with equals, he was still a decent fellow, and, in a way, by no means stupid. But whenever he found himself among those who were below him—even a single rank—he became impossible. He fell silent and was quite pitiable, because even he himself realized that he could have been having a much better time. Sometimes he was obviously longing to join some group in a lively conversation, but he would be stopped by the thought that he would be going too far, putting himself on familiar terms and thereby losing face. And so he remained eternally in silent, aloof isolation, only occasionally uttering some monosyllabic sounds, and, as a result, he acquired a reputation as a deadly bore.

It was to this important personage that Akaky Akakievich presented himself, and at a most unpropitious moment to boot. That is, very unpropitious for him, although quite suitable for the important personage. The latter was in his office talking gaily to a childhood friend who had recently come to Petersburg and whom he hadn't seen for many years. This was the moment when they announced that there was a man named Shoenik to see him.

"Who's he?" the personage wanted to know.

"Some clerk," they told him.

"I see. Let him wait. I am not available now."

Here it should be noted that the important personage was greatly exaggerating. He was available. He and his friend had talked over everything imaginable. For some time now the conversation had been interlaced with lengthy silences, and they weren't doing much more than slapping each other on the thigh and saying:

"So that's how it is, Ivan Abramovich."

"Yes, indeed, Stepan Varlamovich!"

Still Akaky Akakievich had to wait, so that his friend, who had left the government service long ago and now lived in the country, could see what a long time employees had to wait in his reception room.

At last, when they had talked and had sat silent facing each other for as long as they could stand it, when they had smoked a cigar reclining in comfortable armchairs with sloping backs, the important personage, as if he had just recalled it, said to his secretary who was standing at the door with papers for a report:

"Wait a minute. Wasn't there a clerk waiting? Tell him to come in."

Seeing Akaky Akakievich's humble appearance and his wretched old frock coat, he turned abruptly to face him and said: "What do you want?"

He spoke in the hard, sharp voice which he had deliberately developed by practicing at home before a mirror an entire week before he had taken over his present exalted position.

Akaky Akakievich, who had felt properly subdued even before this, felt decidedly embarrassed. He did his best, as far as he could control his tongue, to explain what had happened. Of course, he added even more than his usual share of phrases like "that is to say" and "so to speak." The overcoat, he explained, was completely new and had been cruelly taken away from him and he had turned to the important personage, that is to say, come to him, in the hope that he would, so to speak, intercede for him somehow, that is to say, write to the Superintendent of Police or, so to speak, to someone, and find the overcoat.

For some unimaginable reason the important personage found his manner too familiar.

"My dear sir," he answered sharply, "don't you know the proper channels? Do you realize whom you're addressing and what the proper procedure should be? You should first have handed in a petition to the office. It would have gone to the head clerk. From him it would have reached the section head, who would have approached my secretary and only then would the secretary have presented it to me. . . ."

"But, Your Excellency," said Akaky Akakievich, trying to gather what little composure he had and feeling at the same time that he was sweating terribly, "I, Your Excellency, ventured to trouble you because secretaries, that is to say . . . are, so to speak, an unreliable lot. . . ."

"What, what, what?" demanded the important personage. "Where did you pick up such an attitude? Where did you get such ideas? What is this insubordination that is spreading among young people against their chiefs and superiors?"

The important personage, apparently, had not noticed that Akaky Akakievich was well over fifty. Thus, surely, if he could be called young at all it would only be relatively, that is, to someone of seventy.

"Do you realize to whom you are talking? Do you appreciate who I am? Do you really realize, do you, I'm asking you?"

Here he stamped his foot and raised his voice to such a pitch that there was no need to be an Akaky Akakievich to be frightened.

And Akaky Akakievich froze completely. He staggered, his whole body shook, and he was quite unable to keep his feet. If a messenger hadn't rushed over and supported him, he would

have collapsed onto the floor. They carried him out almost unconscious.

And the important personage, pleased to see that his dramatic effect had exceeded his expectations, and completely delighted with the idea that a word from him could knock a man unconscious, glanced at his friend to see what he thought of it all and was pleased to see that the friend looked somewhat at a loss and that fear had extended to him too.

Akaky Akakievich remembered nothing about getting downstairs and out into the street. He could feel neither hand nor foot. In all his life he had never been so severely reprimanded by a high official, and not a direct chief of his at that. He walked open-mouthed through a blizzard, again and again stumbling off the sidewalk. The wind, according to Petersburg custom, blew at him from all four sides at once, out of every side street. In no time it had blown him a sore throat and he got himself home at last quite unable to say a word. His throat was swollen and he went straight to bed. That's how severe the effects of an adequate reprimand can be.

The next day he was found to have a high fever. Thanks to the generous assistance of the Petersburg climate, the illness progressed beyond all expectations. A doctor came, felt his pulse, found there was nothing he could do and prescribed a poultice. That was done so that the patient would not be deprived of the beneficial aid of medicine. The doctor added, however, that, by the way, the patient had another day and a half to go, after which he would be what is called kaput. Then, turning to the landlady, the doctor said:

"And you, my good woman, I'd not waste my time if I were you. I'd order him the coffin right away. A pine one. The oak ones, I imagine, would be too expensive for him."

Whether Akaky Akakievich heard what for him were fateful words, and, if he heard, whether they had a shattering effect on him and whether he was sorry to lose his wretched life, are matters of conjecture. He was feverish and delirious the whole time. Apparitions, each stranger than the last, kept crowding before him. He saw Petrovich and ordered an overcoat containing some sort of concealed traps to catch the thieves who were hiding under his bed, so that every minute he kept calling his landlady to come and pull out the one who had even slipped under his blanket. Next, he would ask why his old dressing gown was

hanging there in front of him when he had a new overcoat. Then he would find himself standing before the important personage, listening to the reprimand and repeating over and over: "I am sorry, Your Excellency, I am sorry."

Then he began to swear, using the most frightful words, which caused his old landlady to cross herself in horror; never in her life had she heard anything like it from him, and what made it even worse was that they came pouring out on the heels of the phrase, "Your Excellency." After that he talked complete nonsense and it was impossible to make out anything he was saying, except that his disconnected words kept groping for that lost overcoat of his. Then, at last, poor Akaky Akakievich gave up the ghost.

They did not bother to seal his room or his belongings because there were no heirs and, moreover, very little to inherit—namely, a bundle of goose quills, a quire of white government paper, three pairs of socks, a few buttons that had come off his trousers, and the old dressing-gown coat already mentioned. God knows whom they went to; even the reporter of this story did not care enough to find out.

They took Akaky Akakievich away and buried him. And Petersburg went on without him exactly as if he had never existed. A creature had vanished, disappeared. He had had no one to protect him. No one had ever paid him the slightest attention. Not even that which a naturalist pays to a common fly which he mounts on a pin and looks at through his microscope. True, this creature, who had meekly borne the office jokes and gone quietly to his grave, had had, toward the end of his life, a cherished visitor—the overcoat, which for a brief moment had brightened his wretched existence. Then a crushing blow had finished everything, a blow such as befalls the powerful of the earth. . . .

A few days after his death, a messenger from his office was sent to his lodgings with an order summoning him to report immediately; the chief was asking for him. But the messenger had to return alone and to report that Akaky Akakievich could not come.

"Why not?" he was asked.

"Because," the messenger said, "he died. They buried him four days ago."

That is how the department found out about Akaky Akakievich's death, and the next day a new clerk sat in his place: he was much taller and his handwriting was not as straight. In fact, his letters slanted considerably.

But who would have imagined that that was not the end of Akaky Akakievich, that he was fated to live on and make his presence felt for a few days after his death as if in compensation for having spent his life unnoticed by anyone? But that's the way it happened and our little story gains an unexpectedly fantastic ending. Rumors suddenly started to fly around Petersburg that a ghost was haunting the streets at night in the vicinity of the Kalinkin Bridge. The ghost, which looked like a little clerk, was purportedly searching for a stolen overcoat and used this pretext to pull the coats off the shoulders of everyone he met without regard for rank or title. And it made no difference what kind of coat it was—cat, beaver, fox, bearskin, in fact any of the furs and skins people have thought up to cover their own skins with.

One of the department employees saw the ghost with his own eyes and instantly recognized Akaky Akakievich. However, he was so terrified that he dashed off as fast as his legs would carry him and so didn't get a good look; he only saw from a distance that the ghost was shaking his finger at him. Complaints kept pouring in, and not only from petty employees, which would have been understandable. One and all, even Privy Councilors, were catching chills in their backs and shoulders from having their overcoats peeled off. The police were ordered to catch the ghost at any cost, dead or alive, and to punish him with due severity as a warning to others. And what's more, they nearly succeeded.

To be precise, a watchman caught the ghost red-handed, grabbed it by the collar, in Kiryushkin Alley, as it was trying to pull the coat off a retired musician who, in his day, used to tootle on the flute. Grabbing it, he called for help from two colleagues of his and asked them to hold on to it for just a minute. He had, he said, to get his snuffbox out of his boot so that he could bring some feeling back to his nose, which had been frostbitten six times in his life. But it was evidently snuff that even a ghost couldn't stand. The man, closing his right nostril with his finger, had hardly sniffed up half a fistful into the left when the ghost sneezed so violently that the three watchmen were blinded by the resulting shower. They all raised their fists to wipe their eyes and, when they could see again, the ghost had vanished. They even wondered whether they had really held him at all. After that, watchmen were so afraid of the ghost that they felt reluctant to interfere with live robbers and contented themselves with shouting from a distance: "Hey you! On your way!"

And the clerk's ghost began to haunt the streets well beyond the Kalinkin Bridge, spreading terror among the meek.

However, we have completely neglected the important personage, who really, in a sense, was the cause of the fantastic direction that this story—which, by the way, is completely true—has taken. First of all, it is only fair to say that, shortly after poor Akaky Akakievich, reduced to a pulp, had left his office, the important personage felt a twinge of regret. Compassion was not foreign to him—many good impulses stirred his heart, although his position usually prevented them from coming to the surface. As soon as his visiting friend had left the office, his thoughts returned to Akaky Akakievich. And after that, almost every day, he saw in his mind's eye the bloodless face of the little clerk who had been unable to take a proper reprimand. This thought was so disturbing that a week later he went so far as to send a clerk from his office to see how Akaky Akakievich was doing and to find out whether, in fact, there was any way to help him. And when he heard the news that Akaky Akakievich had died suddenly of a fever, it was almost a blow to him, even made him feel guilty and spoiled his mood for the whole day.

Trying to rid himself of these thoughts, to forget the whole unpleasant business, he went to a party at a friend's house. There he found himself in respectable company and, what's more, among people nearly all of whom were of the same standing so that there was absolutely nothing to oppress him. A great change came over him. He let himself go, chatted pleasantly, was amiable, in a word, spent a very pleasant evening. At supper, he drank a couple of glasses of champagne, a well-recommended prescription for inducing good spirits. The champagne gave him an inclination for something special and so he decided not to go home but instead to pay a little visit to a certain well-known lady named Karolina Ivanovna, a lady, it seems, of German extraction, toward whom he felt very friendly. It should be said that the important personage was no longer a young man, that he was a good husband, the respected father of a family. His two sons, one of whom already had a civil-service post, and his sweet-faced sixteen-year-old daughter, who had a slightly hooked but nevertheless pretty little nose, greeted him every day with a "Bonjour, Papa." His wife, a youngish woman and not unattractive at that, gave him her hand to kiss and then kissed his. But although the important personage was quite content with these displays of family affection, he considered it the proper thing to do to have, for friendship's sake, a lady friend in another part of the city. This lady friend was not a bit prettier or younger than his wife, but the world is full of such puzzling things and it is not our business to judge them.

So the important personage came down the steps, stepped into his sledge, and said to the coachman:

"To Karolina Ivanovna's."

Wrapping his warm luxurious fur coat around him, he sat back in his seat. He was in that state so cherished by Russians, in which, without your having to make any effort, thoughts, each one pleasanter than the last, slip into your head by themselves.

Perfectly content, he went over all the most pleasant moments at the party, over the clever retorts that had caused that select gathering to laugh. He even repeated many of them under his breath and, still finding them funny, laughed heartily at them all over again, which was natural enough. However, he kept being bothered by gusts of wind which would suddenly blow, God knows from where or for what reasons, cutting his face, throwing lumps of snow into it, filling the cape of his coat like a sail and throwing it over his head, so that he had to extricate himself from it again and again.

Suddenly the important personage felt someone grab him violently from behind. He turned around and saw a small man in a worn-out frock coat. Terrified, he recognized Akaky Akakievich, his face as white as the snow and looking altogether very ghostly indeed. Fear took over completely when the important personage saw the ghost's mouth twist and, sending a whiff of the grave into his face, utter the following words:

"I've caught you at last. I've got you by the collar now! It's the coat I need. You did nothing about mine and hollered at me to boot. Now I'll take yours!"

The poor important personage almost died. He may have displayed force of character in the office and, in general, toward his inferiors, so that after one glance at his strong face and manly figure, people would say: "Quite a man," but now, like many other mighty-looking people, he was so frightened that he began to think, and not without reason, that he was about to have an attack of something or other. He was even very helpful in peeling off his coat, after which he shouted to the coachman in a ferocious tone:

"Home! As fast as you can!"

The coachman, hearing the ferocious tone which the important personage used in critical moments and which was sometimes accompanied with something even more drastic, instinctively ducked his head and cracked his whip, so that they tore away like a streak. In a little over six minutes the important personage was in front of his house. Instead of being at Karolina Ivanovna's, he was somehow staggering to his room, pale, terrified, and coatless. There he spent such a restless night that the next morning, at breakfast, his daughter said:

"You look terribly pale this morning, Papa."

But Papa was silent, and he didn't say a word to anyone about what had happened to him, or where he had been or where he had intended to go. This incident made a deep impression upon him. From then on his subordinates heard far less often: "How dare you!" and "Do you know whom you're talking to?" And even when he did use these expressions it was after listening to what others had to say.

But even more remarkable—after that night, Akaky Akakievich's ghost was never seen again. The important personage's overcoat must have fitted him snugly. At any rate, one no longer heard of coats being torn from people's shoulders. However, many busybodies wouldn't let the matter rest there and maintained that the ghost was still haunting certain distant parts of the city. And, sure enough, a watchman in the Kolomna district caught a glimpse of the ghost behind a house. But he was rather a frail watchman. (Once an ordinary, but mature, piglet, rushing out of a private house, knocked him off his feet to the huge delight of a bunch of cabbies, whom he fined two kopeks each for their lack of respect—then he spent the proceeds on tobacco.) So, being rather frail, the watchman didn't dare to arrest the ghost. Instead he followed it in the darkness until at last it stopped suddenly, turned to face him, and asked:

"You looking for trouble?"

And it shook a huge fist at him, much larger than any you'll find among the living.

"No," the watchman said, turning away.

This ghost, however, was a much taller one and wore an enormous mustache. It walked off, it seems, in the direction of the Obukhov Bridge and soon dissolved into the gloom of night.

The Downeaster "Alexa"

Billy Joel

Well I'm on the Downeaster "Alexa"
And I'm cruising through Block Island Sound
I have chartered a course to the Vineyard
But tonight I am Nantucket bound

We took on diesel back in Montauk yesterday
And left this morning from the bell in Gardner's Bay
Like all the locals here I've had to sell my home
Too proud to leave I worked my fingers to the bone

So I could own my Downeaster "Alexa"
And I go where the ocean is deep
There are giants out there in the canyons
And a good captain can't fall asleep

I've got bills to pay and children who need clothes
I know there's fish out there but where God only knows
They say these waters aren't what they used to be
But I've got people back on land who count on me

So if you see my Downeaster "Alexa"
And if you work with the rod and the reel
Tell my wife I am trolling Atlantis
And I still have my hands on the wheel

Now I drive my Downeaster "Alexa"
More and more miles from shore every year
Since they told me I can't sell no stripers
And there's no luck in swordfishing here

I was a bayman like my father was before
Can't make a living as a bayman anymore
There ain't much future for a man who works the sea
But there ain't no island left for islanders like me

Growth

Philip Levine

In the soap factory where I worked
when I was fourteen, I spoke to
no one and only one man spoke
to me and then to command me
to wheel the little cars of damp chips
into the ovens. While the chips dried
I made more racks, nailing together
wood lath and ordinary screening
you'd use to keep flies out, racks
and more racks each long afternoon,
for this was a growing business
in a year of growth. The oil drums
of fat would arrive each morning,
too huge for me to tussle with,
reeking of the dark, cavernous
kitchens of the Greek and Rumanian
restaurants, of cheap hamburger joints,
White Towers and worse. They would
sulk in the battered yard behind
the plant until my boss, Leo,
the squat Ukrainian dollied them in
to become, somehow, through the magic
of chemistry, pure soap. My job
was always the racks and the ovens—
two low ceilinged metal rooms
the color of sick skin. When I
slid open the heavy doors my eyes
started open, the pores
of my skull shrivelled, and sweat
smelling of scared animal burst from
me everywhere. Head down I entered,
first to remove what had dried
and then to wheel in the damp, raw
yellow curls of new soap, grained
like iris petals or unseamed quartz.
Then out to the open weedy yard

among the waiting and emptied drums
where I hammered and sawed, singing
my new life of working and earning,
outside in the fresh air of Detroit
in 1942, a year of growth.

Assembly Line

Shu Ting

Translated by Carolyn Kizer

In time's assembly line
Night presses against night.
We come off the factory night-shift
In line as we march towards home.
Over our heads in a row
The assembly line of stars
Stretches across the sky.
Beside us, little trees
Stand numb in assembly lines.

The stars must be exhausted
After thousands of years
Of journeys which never change.
The little trees are all sick,
Choked on smog and monotony,
Stripped of their color and shape.
It's not hard to feel for them;
We share the same tempo and rhythm.

Yes, I'm numb to my own existence
As if, like the trees and stars
—perhaps just out of habit
—perhaps just out of sorrow,
I'm unable to show concern
For my own manufactured fate.

Those Winter Sundays

Robert Hayden

Sundays too my father got up early
and put his clothes on in the blueblack cold,
then with cracked hands that ached
from labor in the weekday weather made
banked fires blaze. No one ever thanked him.

I'd wake and hear the cold splintering, breaking.
When the rooms were warm, he'd call,
and slowly I would rise and dress,
fearing the chronic angers of that house,

Speaking indifferently to him,
who had driven out the cold
and polished my good shoes as well.
What did I know, what did I know
of love's austere and lonely offices?

The Use of Force

William Carlos Williams

THEY were new patients to me, all I had was the name, Olson. Please come down as soon as you can, my daughter is very sick.

When I arrived I was met by the mother, a big startled looking woman, very clean and apologetic who merely said, Is this the doctor? and let me in. In the back, she added. You must excuse us, doctor, we have her in the kitchen where it is warm. It is very damp here sometimes.

The child was fully dressed and sitting on her father's lap near the kitchen table. He tried to get up, but I motioned for him not to bother, took off my overcoat and started to look things over. I could see that they were all very nervous, eyeing me up and down distrustfully. As often, in such cases, they weren't telling me more than they had to, it was up to me to tell them; that's why they were spending three dollars on me.

The child was fairly eating me up with her cold, steady eyes, and no expression to her face whatever. She did not move and seemed, inwardly, quiet; an unusually attractive little thing, and as strong as a heifer in appearance. But her face was flushed, she was breathing rapidly, and I realized that she had a high fever. She had magnificent blonde hair, in profusion. One of those picture children often reproduced in advertising leaflets and the photogravure sections of the Sunday papers.

She's had a fever for three days, began the father and we don't know what it comes from. My wife has given her things, you know, like people do, but it don't do no good. And there's been a lot of sickness around. So we tho't you'd better look her over and tell us what is the matter.

As doctors often do I took a trial shot at it as a point of departure. Has she had a sore throat?

Both parents answered me together, No . . . No, she says her throat don't hurt her.

Does your throat hurt you? added the mother to the child. But the little girl's expression didn't change nor did she move her eyes from my face.

Have you looked?

I tried to, said the mother, but I couldn't see.

As it happens we have been having a number of cases of diphtheria in the school to which this child went during that month and we were all, quite apparently, thinking of that, though no one had as yet spoken of the thing.

Well, I said, suppose we take a look at the throat first. I smiled in my best professional manner and asking for the child's first name I said, come on, Mathilda, open your mouth and let's take a look at your throat.

Nothing doing.

Aw, come on, I coaxed, just open your mouth wide and let me take a look. Look, I said opening both hands wide, I haven't anything in my hands. Just open up and let me see.

Such a nice man, put in the mother. Look how kind he is to you. Come on, do what he tells you to. He won't hurt you.

At that I ground my teeth in disgust. If only they wouldn't use the word "hurt" I might be able to get somewhere. But I did not allow myself to be hurried or disturbed but speaking quietly and slowly I approached the child again.

As I moved my chair a little nearer suddenly with one catlike movement both her hands clawed instinctively for my eyes and she almost reached them too. In fact she knocked my glasses flying and they fell, though unbroken, several feet away from me on the kitchen floor.

Both the mother and father almost turned themselves inside out in embarrassment and apology. You bad girl, said the mother, taking her and shaking her by one arm. Look what you've done. The nice man . . .

For heaven's sake, I broke in. Don't call me a nice man to her. I'm here to look at her throat on the chance that she might have diphtheria and possibly die of it. But that's nothing to her. Look here, I said to the child, we're going to look at your throat. You're old enough to understand what I'm saying. Will you open it now by yourself or shall we have to open it for you?

Not a move. Even her expression hadn't changed. Her breaths however were coming faster and faster. Then the battle began. I had to do it. I had to have a throat culture for her own protection. But first I told the parents that it was entirely up to them. I explained the danger but said that I would not insist on a throat examination so long as they would take the responsibility.

If you don't do what the doctor says you'll have to go to the hospital, the mother admonished her severely.

Oh yeah? I had to smile to myself. After all, I had already fallen in love with the savage brat, the parents were contemptible to me. In the ensuing struggle they grew more and more abject, crushed, exhausted while she surely rose to magnificent heights of insane fury of effort bred of her terror of me.

The father tried his best, and he was a big man but the fact that she was his daughter, his shame at her behavior and his dread of hurting her made him release her just at the critical moment several times when I had almost achieved success, till I wanted to kill him. But his dread also that she might have diphtheria made him tell me to go on, go on though he himself was almost fainting, while the mother moved back and forth behind us raising and lowering her hands in an agony of apprehension.

Put her in front of you on your lap, I ordered, and hold both her wrists.

But as soon as he did the child let out a scream. Don't, you're hurting me. Let go of my hands. Let them go I tell you. Then she shrieked terrifyingly, hysterically. Stop it! Stop it! You're killing me!

Do you think she can stand it, doctor! said the mother.

You get out, said the husband to his wife. Do you want her to die of diphtheria?

Come on now, hold her, I said.

Then I grasped the child's head with my left hand and tried to get the wooden tongue depressor between her teeth. She fought, with clenched teeth, desperately! But now I also had grown furious—at a child. I tried to hold myself down but I couldn't. I know how to expose a throat for inspection. And I did my best. When finally I got the wooden spatula behind the last teeth and just the point of it into the mouth cavity, she opened up for an instant but before I could see anything she came down again and gripping the wooden blade between her molars she reduced it to splinters before I could get it out again.

Aren't you ashamed, the mother yelled at her. Aren't you ashamed to act like that in front of the doctor?

Get me a smooth-handled spoon of some sort, I told the mother. We're going through with this. The child's mouth was already bleeding. Her tongue was cut and she was screaming in wild hysterical shrieks. Perhaps I should have desisted and come back in an hour or more. No doubt it would have been better. But I have seen at least two children lying dead in bed of neglect in such cases, and feeling that I must get a diagnosis now or never I went at it again. But the worst of it was that I too had got beyond reason. I could have torn the child apart in my own fury and enjoyed it. It was a pleasure to attack her. My face was burning with it.

The damned little brat must be protected against her own idiocy, one says to one's self at such times. Others must be protected against her. It is a social necessity. And all these things are true. But a blind fury, a feeling of adult shame, bred of a longing for muscular release are the operatives. One goes on to the end.

In a final unreasoning assault I overpowered the child's neck and jaws. I forced the heavy silver spoon back of her teeth and down her throat till she gagged. And there it was—both tonsils covered with membrane. She had fought valiantly to keep me from knowing her secret. She had been hiding that sore throat for three days at least and lying to her parents in order to escape just such an outcome as this.

Now truly she *was* furious. She had been on the defensive before but now she attacked. Tried to get off her father's lap and fly at me while tears of defeat blinded her eyes.

The Ballad of John Henry

Traditional

John Henry was a little baby boy
You could hold him in the palm of your hand.
He gave a long and lonesome cry,
"Gonna be a steel-drivin' man, Lawd, Lawd,
Gonna be a steel-drivin' man."

They took John Henry to the tunnel,
Put him in the lead to drive,
The rock was so tall, John Henry so small,
That he laid down his hammer and he cried, "Lawd, Lawd,"
Laid down his hammer and he cried.

John Henry started on the right hand,
The steam drill started on the left,
"Fo' I'd let that steam drill beat me down,
I'd hammer my fool self to death, Lawd, Lawd,
Hammer my fool self to death."

John Henry told his captain,
"A man ain't nothin' but a man,
Fo' I let your steam drill beat me down
I'll die with this hammer in my hand, Lawd, Lawd,
Die with this hammer in my hand."

Now the captain told John Henry,
"I believe my tunnel's sinkin' in."
"Stand back, Captain, and doncha be afraid,
That's nothin' but my hammer catchin' wind, Lawd, Lawd,
That's nothin' but my hammer catchin' wind."

John Henry told his cap'n,
"Look yonder, boy, what do I see?
Your drill's done broke and your hole's done choke,
And you can't drive steel like me, Lawd, Lawd,
You can't drive steel like me."

John Henry hammerin' in the mountain,
Til the handle of his hammer caught on fire,
He drove so hard till he broke his po' heart,
Then he laid down his hammer and he died, Lawd, Lawd,
He laid down his hammer and he died.

They took John Henry to the tunnel,
And they buried him in the sand,
An' every locomotive come rollin' by
Say, "There lies a steel-drivin' man, Lawd, Lawd,
There lies a steel-drivin' man."

Biographical Notes

Ann Arnott Ann Arnott is well known as one of the few female automotive journalists for major consumer publications. Ongoing columns include "Woman at the Wheel" for *Woman's Day* magazine, "A Woman's Spin" in the *Detroit Free Press*, and a twice-a-month column in the *New York Post*.

David Herring (born 1964) Born in North Carolina, Herring now resides near Annapolis, Maryland, with his wife, Michele, and their newborn son, Drew. David currently works for NASA's Goddard Space Flight Center in Greenbelt, Maryland. As such, he utilizes his educational backgrounds in journalism, science and technical writing, and science education to communicate to the general public the goals and objectives of NASA's Earth Observing System missions. The EOS-AM satellite, launched in 1998, will be the most technologically advanced space-based remote sensor for quantifying the causes and effects of climate change on both global and regional scales.

Dianne Hales and Lt. Col. Robert E. Hales, M.D. Dianne and Robert Hales combine their talents to write articles like the one included in this anthology. The medical training of Dr. Hales and the writing talents of the widely published Dianne Hales help them write articles on a variety of medical topics. Dr. Robert Hales has written more than one hundred scientific articles and book chapters, as well as fourteen books. Dianne Hales is one of the most widely published freelance writers in the country. Her works have been translated into French, German, Italian, Spanish, Swedish, and Portuguese.

Craig R. Whitney (born 1943) Whitney traveled to Vietnam as a U.S. Navy lieutenant from 1966 through 1969. Later, during his more than twenty-five years with *The New York Times*, he served as bureau chief in Saigon, Bonn, Moscow, Washington, and London. He lives in Bonn with his wife and two children.

Hy Hammer As a retired chief of the Examining Service Division for the New York City Department of Personnel, Hy Hammer knows a lot about civil service requirements. In his book *The Civil Service Handbook*, he offers tips on successfully applying for a civil service job. In addition, he includes a wide range of job descriptions for potential applicants to consider.

Cary Bricker As a legal aid in New York City, Cary Bricker works behind the scenes as well as in the courtroom. She uses her writing skills to prepare summations and briefs of criminal cases.

E! Online This home page is the electronic version of the popular television program *E!* The page has links to entertainment news and up-to-the-minute information on movies, music, and celebrities.

Roger Ebert (born 1942) Thumbs up, thumbs down—these indications of a movie's quality were made popular by the duo of Siskel and Ebert, Chicago-based movie reviewers and co-hosts of their own television program. Roger Ebert's reviews appear in the *Chicago Sun-Times* and more than two hundred other newspapers around the country. He has won two Pulitzer Prizes for his work. About movie viewing he has said: "The audience: In the dark, lined up facing the screen. The light comes from behind their heads—from back there where dreams come true."

Jetsun Pema (born 1940) A woman of amazing strength and vision, Jetsun Pema is known as "The Mother of Tibet." Like many Tibetans, including the Dalai Lama, she lives in exile in Dharamsala, India. Although she is forced to live far from her native land, she is dedicated to keeping Tibetan culture alive. She heads the Tibetan Children's Village, which educates exiled Tibetan children about their culture and religion. She is also active in politics; she was the first woman to serve as a minister in the exiled Tibetan government. In her autobiography, *Tibet: My Story,* she shares insights into her life as the Dalai Lama's sister.

Terry Gross The National Public Radio program *Fresh Air With Terry Gross* has received a number of awards. One reason may be Gross's intelligent, thoughtful interview style. She puts her guests at ease, which leads them to share insights and information that are fresh and surprising. Gross began her radio career in 1973, working at a public radio station in Buffalo, New York. In 1985, the first *Fresh Air* was produced as a weekly half-hour show. Since then, the show has evolved into a one-hour national edition, airing on 160 stations.

William A. Nolen (1928–1986) In his book *The Making of a Surgeon,* William A. Nolen shares the excitement and anxiety of his experiences as an intern and resident in the 1950's at Bellevue

Hospital in New York. His book caused quite a stir in the medical community: Because it revealed the good and bad details behind the scenes at a hospital, many doctors felt that Nolen had betrayed the medical profession. Nolen, however, felt that medicine should not be shrouded in mystery and went on to write other books, including *A Surgeon's World* and *Surgeon Under the Knife*.

Michael Dorris (1945–1997) His Native American heritage was an important influence for Michael Dorris. Although he earned one degree in English and another in the history of theater, his interest in his Modoc ancestry led him into the field of cultural anthropology. He served as chairman of Native American Studies at Dartmouth College. As a writer, Dorris created poetry, short stories, novels, songs, essays, and reviews.

Maya Angelou (born 1928) Maya Angelou was born Marguerite Johnson in St. Louis, Missouri. Her difficult childhood, in Arkansas and California, became the source for her extremely popular autobiography, *I Know Why the Caged Bird Sings.* Her experiences as a civil rights worker, a singer, and an actress have all contributed to her view of life. She shares some of her philosophy in the book *Wouldn't Take Nothin' for My Journey Now,* a collection of essays.

Studs Terkel (born 1912) A born interviewer, Studs Terkel originally studied law. Later he worked as an actor and a movie theater manager. Hosting a variety of radio and television interview programs led Terkel into the work for which he is most famous. With his tape recorder, Terkel enters the lives of ordinary people. From taped conversations, he creates thoughtful verbal portraits of the people he interviews.

S. J. Perelman (1904–1979) Finding the humor in life was the key to Perelman's success as a screenwriter and freelance writer. His film credits include two Marx Brothers films, *Monkey Business* and *Horse Feathers.* During his fifty-year career, he contributed to a number of magazines, most notably *The New Yorker,* in which his work appeared regularly.

Charles Edison As the son of the famous inventor, Charles Edison captures intimate details of his father's life and personality that other writers could not. Charles was the son of Thomas Edison and his second wife, Mina. (Thomas Edison's first wife,

Mary Stilwell, died in 1884.) As an adult, Charles served as secretary of the navy and governor of New Jersey.

Trudy Pax Farr Growing up on a farm in Celina, Ohio, prepared Farr for hard work as an adult. In addition to her work in a steel mill, Farr has also worked as an instructor, teaching English as a second language. Today, Farr lives in Minnesota, working as a freelance writer.

Michael Jordan (born 1963) This basketball superstar was cut from his high-school team in his sophomore year. His natural ability and perseverance later helped him to establish himself as one of the greatest basketball players of all time. He has led his team to numerous NBA championships and has won many individual awards. He is almost as well known for his positive attitude as he is for his incredible talent.

Homer Ancient Greeks regarded Homer as their first and greatest poet. He is widely acknowledged as the author of the *Iliad* and the *Odyssey*, but little else is known about him. Seven cities—Chios, Colphon, Smyrna, Rhodes, Argos, Athens, and Salamis—claim to have been his birthplace.

Alan Jackson (born 1958) As a mechanic's son, Alan Jackson was at first more interested in tinkering with cars than he was in playing music. He learned to play the guitar while in his teens, but at the time saw music more as a hobby than a career. After receiving some local attention during the 1980's, Jackson moved to Nashville to try his hand in the country music business. His debut album, *Here in the Real World*, went gold in 1990, establishing Jackson as a solid presence in the country music scene.

Martín Espada (born 1957) Born and raised in Brooklyn, Espada has held a number of jobs that have given him background for his work-related poems. As a desk clerk in a transient hotel, a welfare rights paralegal, a groundskeeper at a minor league ballpark, and a bindery worker in a printing plant, he has seen the ups and downs of the working-class life he writes about.

Robert Frost (1874–1963) Frost was born in San Francisco but moved to New England, his family's original home, when he was eleven. In his youth, he worked as a farmer, editor, and schoolteacher, absorbing the ebb and flow of New England life that would form the themes for many of his poems. Encouraged by the famous poets Ezra Pound and William Butler Yeats, Frost published his first volume of poetry, *A Boy's Will,* in 1913. He went on to become one of the most successful and prolific poets the country has ever known, winning numerous awards, including four Pulitzer Prizes.

Nikolai Gogol (1809–1852) During his short life, Nikolai Gogol (nē′ kô lī gō′ gəl) established himself as one of the finest and most influential Russian writers of the nineteenth century. Gogol was born in the Ukraine, the son of a landowner. As a teenager, he suffered from feelings of isolation and discontent and turned to writing as a means of expressing these emotions. He published his first collection of short stories, *Evenings on a Farm Near Dikanka,* in 1832. His most famous short story is "The Overcoat," published in 1842. Because of his grimly accurate portrayal of nineteenth-century Russian life, Gogol has come to be regarded as the founder of Russian Realism.

Billy Joel (born 1949) The son of Jewish immigrants, Billy Joel grew up in Hicksville, New York. At sixteen, he became the pianist for a local band. With the money he earned, he helped his struggling family pay the mortgage on their house. As a solo artist, Joel's first album did not bring him fame or fortune. Commercial success came with the release of *Piano Man.* Since then, he has explored a wide variety of themes, issues, and styles in his music.

Philip Levine (born 1928) As a young man, Levine worked in an automobile assembly plant and was a member of several labor unions. Although he began teaching English when he was thirty, his poetry reflects his early work on the railroads and in factories. His poetry collection *What Work Is* won a National Book Award for poetry.

Shu Ting (born 1952) As a teenager, Chinese poet Shu Ting was forced by political events to leave Beijing and live in a small peasant village. She gained fame as a poet while still in her twenties. In 1981 and 1983, she won China's National Poetry Award. Today, she makes her home in the seaport city of Xiamen.

Robert Hayden (1913–1980) An extremely versatile poet, Robert Hayden used a variety of poetic forms and techniques and focused on a wide range of subjects. In addition to writing about his personal experiences, Hayden wrote about current and historical events, mythology, and folklore. He was born in Detroit and attended schools in Michigan and Tennessee. His award-winning poetry includes the collection *A Ballad of Remembrance.*

William Carlos Williams (1883–1963) Most people would agree that being a doctor is a full-time job. William Carlos Williams, however, was both a doctor and a poet. When asked how he managed his double career, he replied that he treated his patients like poems and his poems like patients. Williams believed that Americans should write about the details in the world around them.

Acknowledgments

Harold Ober Associates Incorporated
  "Insert Flap 'A' and Throw Away" by S. J. Perelman. First published in
The New Yorker. Copyright © 1944 by S. J. Perelman. Copyright renewed
1972 by S. J. Perelman. Reprinted by permission of Harold Ober Associates,
Incorporated.

Prentice Hall, Inc.
  "Summation for a Jury" by Cary Bricker, commissioned for Prentice Hall
Writer's Solution Sourcebook, Diamond. Copyright © 1998 by Prentice Hall,
Inc. Reprinted by permission of Prentice Hall, Inc.

Random House, Inc.
  "First Job" from *I Know Why the Caged Bird Sings* by Maya Angelou.
Copyright © 1969 by Maya Angelou and renewed 1997 by Maya Angelou.
Reprinted by permission of Random House, Inc.

Reader's Digest
  "It's Plain Hard Work That Does It" (originally entitled "My Most Unforgettable Character: Thomas Edison") by Charles Edison is reprinted with permission from the December 1961 *Reader's Digest.* Copyright © 1961 by the
Reader's Digest Association, Inc.

Scripps Howard News Service
  "Mel Allen: Portrait of a Sportscaster" from MLB Features/New York Yan-
kees Features Page/The New York Yankees Page/The Baseball Server. © 1996
Copyright Nando.net, 1996 Scripps Howard.

Seal Press
  "Steelworker" by Trudy Pax Farr. Reprinted with permission of the pub-
lisher from *Hard-Hatted Women: Stories of Struggle and Success in the
Trades*, edited by Molly Martin (Seattle: Seal Press, 1988).

University of Chicago Press
  Excerpt from *The Iliad of Homer*, translated by Richmond Lattimore. Copyright © 1951, The University of Chicago. Reprinted by permission of the
publisher, University of Chicago Press.

WHYY, Inc.
  "Sister of the Dalai Lama," transcript of radio interview by Terry Gross of
Jetsun Pema on NPR *Fresh Air*, January 23, 1998. Reprinted by permission
of WHYY, Inc.

Warner Chappell
  "Working-class Hero" by Alan Jackson and Don Sampson, from *Don't Rock
the Juke Box.* © 1991 Arista Records, Inc.

John Wiley & Sons, Inc.
  From *175 High-Impact Resumes* by Richard H. Beatty. Copyright © 1996
by Richard H. Beatty. Reprinted by permission of John Wiley & Sons, Inc.

Note: Every effort has been made to locate the copyright owner of material
reprinted in this book. Omissions brought to our attention will be corrected
in subsequent editions.